Power over Life
Leads to Domination of Mankind

Michel Schooyans

Member of the Pontifical Academy of Social Sciences, Consultor to the Pontifical Council on Justice and Peace and to the Pontifical Council for the Family, Dr. Schooyans, philosopher and theologian, is professor of political philosophy as well as social morality and the ethics of demographic problems at the Catholic University of Louvain, Belgium.

Translated by Rev. John H. Miller, C.S.C., S. T. D.

Published by
CENTRAL BUREAU,
Catholic Central Verein of America
3835 Westminster Place
Saint Louis, Missouri 63108

Printed by St. Martin de Porres Lay Dominican Community, New Hope, Kentucky 40052

Prometheus:	"...I have delivered man from his obsession with death."
Coryphaeus:	"What kind of remedy have you discovered, then, for this evil?"
Prometheus:	"I have planted blind hopes in them."
Coryphaeus:	"What strong comfort you have brought to mortals this day!"
Prometheus:	"But I have done more than that: I made them a present of fire."
Coryphaeus:	"What! The flaming fire is now in the hands of ephemerals?"
Prometheus:	"And with it they will learn innumerable arts."
Coryphaeus:	"There you have the grievances for which Zeus..."
Prometheus:	"This disgrace afflicts me without bringing relief to my misfortunes!"
Coryphaeus:	"And no limit was set for your ordeal?"
Prometheus:	"None other than his good pleasure."
Coryphaeus:	"And this good pleasure, whence would it originate? How can you hope for it? Don't you see you've made a mistake? Where was the mistake? I would not like to tell you, it would pain you to hear about it."

From Aeschylus, *Prometheus Bound*.

TABLE OF CONTENTS

It is with great satisfaction that I am able to present to the English-speaking public the work of this superior scholar. Father Schooyans and I originally met at the Human Life International Convention of 1993 in Houston, Texas. I had been asked to assist him in rendering his three addresses for the Convention into more idiomatic English. As we merrily proceeded with our task, we realized that we were very much of the same mind. I also noticed on his desk a small book entitled *Maîtrise de la vie — domination des hommes.*

I interrupted our work without hesitation and began to read sections here and there. I immediately perceived a remarkable piece of work. The sharpness, clarity and depth of his argumentation on this *most crucial question* of our time overwhelmed me. I blurted out without further ado: "Father Michel, I simply must have your permission to translate this into English and publish it. We need this badly here in America!" His response, naturally, came just as unhesitatingly: "That would be a great honor for me. By all means."

The debate in this country has thus far been almost exclusively along the lines of the human life and personhood of the fetus, both demanding absolute respect. Father Schooyans adds thereto and goes on to show unabashedly how undemocratic are those who attack innocent life, massacre thousands of fertilized ova — human embryos — and then, of course, extend their death-dealing technology to the elderly and ill. Yes, undemocratic, for they single out some for death, allowing only some to live. Such power over life and its arbitrary use is typical, not of democracy in which all are of equal dignity, but of despotic totalitarianism which is always self-serving and ignores or tramples underfoot the natural, God-given rights of all human beings.

What he has written applies especially and specifically to the United States with its ever-increasing trend toward governmental control not only over every aspect of our lives but over life itself! With abortion and its cohorts promoted from the highest levels of the federal government, and with more and more state governments jumping on the bandwagon with death-dealing laws, it has become evident that we are fast sliding down the slippery slope of tyranny.

With this attack spreading in ever-widening circles, we can no longer lay claim to being a democracy; we are now in the hands of bureaucrats who, doing the will of those who regard themselves as "masters of life," show utter disregard for the dignity of every human being.

Abortion gives the lie to our democratic pretense; we need to refound not our government, but our Republic!

While expressing my profound gratitude to the genius of our author, I cannot omit a very sincere word of thanks to Rebecca Johnson Nagel, editorial assistant, as well as to Jeanine Smith and Mark Morelli, staff members of the Central Bureau. May their kind grow in number!

John H. Miller, C.S.C.
Translator

This little book sounds an alarm. We shall limit ourselves to discussing very simple matters concerning human life, medical activity, political power, the family, the world of today and that of the future. But this resolve goes against the grain.

These "very simple matters" are being radically called into question by the fantastic achievements in the field of human reproduction on the part of the biomedical sciences these last few years.

Intoxicated by these achievements, all specialties thrown into confusion, our contemporaries sometimes lose their power of discernment and are propelled into a bewitching spiral that leads to the abyss.

From the Renaissance on, an ambiguous relationship was established between science and political power. Today, the biomedical sciences and the techniques they create place powerful instruments of unprecedented effectiveness at the disposal of this world's leaders.

We call *biopolitics* the recourse to science and biomedical techniques in order to govern mankind. Those who have knowledge and know-how in the biomedical domain have at their command a de facto power over mankind.

This very general definition can be made more specific. Biopolitics is also the totality of decisions taken in order to favor certain biomedical research, given its usefulness in governing mankind. Conversely, biopolitics can equally evoke the de facto power that biologists and physicians can exercise over society by reason of their scientific competence. They can exercise this power indirectly through intermediary institutions, or directly on their own authority.

X

Thus a new generation of technocrats is born. Let us call them *biocrats*. They penetrate political institutions or private organizations indifferently — usually both. Their ultimate goal is *to destroy the family and totally and efficiently control the number and quality of human beings.*

Hence, bluntly put, our thesis is that *power over life as actually conceived, leads directly to control over humankind.*

One knows, or at least should be aware of, the role played by biologists and physicians in the rise of Naziism and the consolidation of the regime that ensued.[1] Reports from well informed associations which can hardly be suspected of partiality remind us constantly of the physicians' part in the practice of torture, enforced sterilizations, executions, brainwashing, etc.

Due to the extraordinary attainments mentioned above, we find ourselves in some respects in a situation comparable to the immediate prewar era. At that time, both in Europe and the United States, prominent experts were responsible for phenomenal progress in nuclear physics.

Analyzing what took place in extreme secrecy between the experts and political leaders of the time is beyond the scope of our plan, and, doubtlessly, all has not yet been said on this subject. It is however important to note that in the contracts between the experts and politicians that led to the decision to free the fantastic means indispensable for the making of nuclear weapons, the place given to moral considerations was, at most, very modest. Envisaging the eventual creation of the bomb, Otto Hahn declared that "this would be against the will of God."[2] But this beautiful thought elicited hardly an echo. Research in nuclear physics in fact concentrated on the making of the bomb, and we had to wait for Hiroshima and Nagasaki before America, by then filled with powerless remorse, simultaneously saw the extent of the disaster and felt the overwhelming responsibility for the decisions that led to it. Was that really what the experts and politicians wanted in 1939 and even before?

All the same, the experts paid little attention to the political repercussions that would result from the weapons they had developed. As if the holocausts of Hiroshima and Nagasaki were not enough, the decisions taken in 1939 by President Roosevelt in consultation with the experts were at the origin — not solely, to be sure, but nevertheless directly if distantly — of the impasse in which all discussions on the arms race founder to this day. So true is it that once started, this race is very difficult to stop.

The lesson is clear — at least for those who wish to understand.

To prevent this series of tragedies, to escape from the balance of terror, it was in 1939 and even before that the logic that led to them should have been rejected.

Since then, nevertheless, experts have shown some wisdom in abandoning certain research programs preparing bacteriological warfare. It does honor to their profession and the case is not unique. On May 16,1986, *Le Monde* reported that over six thousand scientists, fifteen of whom were Nobel Prize winners, had resolved not to participate in the research for "Star Wars," also known as "Strategic Defense Initiative."

Hence, the lucid conclusion to be drawn for our purpose is: in matters of biotechnology it is now that the moral problems must be studied; we must now exercise a vision that forecasts the political stakes that have to be anticipated.

Really, the biomedical weapon could in fact cause the nuclear weapon to take second place in the long-term strategies of imperial powers. Nuclear violence — that apart from Hiroshima and Nagasaki is still an eventuality — has been succeeded by biomedical or genetic violence, which is already a reality. To complete it, the ideological violence done to intelligence and will comes to propose an inverse image of reality. In order to make biomedical violence "legitimate," they will deceive public opinion into swallowing the notion that it's all a question of "the new rights of man" and of "promotion of development.' All this is to say that we must without qualification denounce any complicity of violence with lies.

Here are the many reasons that compel us to intervene now and draw attention to the lack of self-regulation in certain scientific circles, to the traffic in information, the excesses of certain political groups, and the greed of certain lobbies.

Michel Schooyans
Louvain-la-Neuve, August 1986
Saint Louis, Mo., July 1993

Endnotes:

[1] See for instance Robert Jay Lifton, *The Nazi Doctors Medical Killing and the Psychology of Genocide*, (New York and London: Macmillan, 1986); Robert N. Proctor, *Medicine Under the Nazi* (Boston: Harvard University Press, 1988).

[2] Regarding to the problems alluded to here, see William Manchester, *The Glory and the Dream. A Narrative History of America*, 1932-1972. 2 vols. (Boston: Little, Brown, 1973-74); see especially vol. 1: 254-261; and Otto Hahn's reaction on p. 255.

chapter I

ABORTION OR DEMOCRACY ON TRIAL

The political dimension of abortion is rarely analyzed in the passionate debates that divide the opinion of our democracies on this question. It is this lack that we would like to make up for in this first chapter, by showing to what extent the liberalization of this practice shakes the very foundations of a democratic society.

It may be surprising at first that an action that targets only individuals could have such far-reaching sociopolitical repercussions, yet such is the case. The reason is simple. It is absolutely impossible for us to put into parentheses the political import of our actions, especially if those actions affect the most fundamental reality of human communities, namely, individual human life. "Man is a political animal," wrote Aristotle in his *Politics* (I, 2). Perhaps we have not yet measured the implications of the adage of antiquity's great philosopher.

1. THE ROMAN MODEL

The Roman citizen was truly a free man: free to come and go as he pleased; free to pursue a career of his choice in the army, law or politics; free to think, to improve himself, to have friendly exchanges. The enjoyment of all these rights was acknowledged as his by custom and law. In practice, the use of these rights was made possible especially through the exploitation of a multitude of slaves. If he was able to travel or devote himself to the delights of leisure and letters, it was because others, between seven and seventy-seven, were constrained to harrowing toil in the fields, in raising cattle, street cleaning, construction, maintenance, transportation, mines, workshops, etc.

Roman citizens exercised their liberty at the expense of thousands of their contemporaries. Large landowners in Latin American and *apparatchiks* in Russia still operate in the same way. That equality is proclaimed means nothing in effect when the constitution is thwarted by regulations — even by laws — and above all by the facts. Stronger people establish their liberty on the ruins of the weaker ones. "The stronger one is never strong enough to remain master forever, unless he transforms his power into a right and obedience to it a duty" (Rousseau, *Social Contract*, I, 3).

Pro-abortion legislation perfectly exemplifies the same dilemma. What liberty is endorsed in effect by the slogan that "abortion will be liberating"? Freedom for the woman, freedom for the man, freedom for society.

Woman has the right to pursue the practice of her profession, the right not to live in an over-crowded apartment, to preserve her reputation, to safeguard her household. . . Man has the right to live the life he desires, to follow his chosen career, to reap the fruits of his effort, to profit from his possessions. . . Society has the right to have a balanced budget enabling it to invest and create jobs, making it possible to promote a life of culture, to maintain an army, to pay thousands of civil servants and teachers, to construct safer roads.

All these rights are real, but in this case a woman claims the exercise of her rights *to the detriment* of the life of the child. At the same time, men and society effectively refuse to help the woman assume the moral and physical responsibility for the child; moreover, they force her to suffer a wound with consequences that will perhaps be dramatic.

The liberal tradition, however, has widely acknowledged the conceived child to be the subject of human rights that deserve special protection. The science of genetics confirms the accuracy of this tradition, since its discoveries oblige us to recognize in the earliest stages of the embryo a being already radically human. Besides, an absolute majority of experts admit this fact, even if they favor abortion (Guttmacher and Potts, for example). Discussions about the mid-term animation or humanization (9, 12, 20 weeks?) again raise a question from medieval times that is surprising to hear among "progressive" people.

2. A CHOICE FOR SOCIETY

Any law liberalizing abortion confirms the idea that "might makes right." This contradicts the whole of our great Western constitutional texts born of centuries of struggle by entire peoples. These people wanted to have recognized an order of justice anterior and superior to the power relationships crystallized in concrete regimes. These people also wanted an order of justice apart from which no concrete regime can enjoy any legitimacy.

What has helped many of the poor throughout history to resist is the awareness that their dignity was as great as that of the powerful, a dignity that had to be recognized despite their weakness. What helped the poor to advance is the awareness of the fundamental dignity of *all* humans, and the profound wickedness involved in asserting the secondary interests of one particular group over the fundamental interests of others.

This consciousness gradually becomes apparent in the democratic ideal of a society that is concerned with the good of all its members; it becomes flesh, at least partially, in the institutions and laws of the Western type; it found a major expression in the 1948 *Universal Declaration of Human Rights* following the 1940-45 cataclysm. Each word in the title of this fundamental text has profound significance. It is a *Declaration* of the rights of man and not an *assigning* of rights to men, because these rights are *naturally* possessed by individuals whether these rights are acknowledged in fact or not; the Declaration is *universal*, because all these rights are possessed by *all* individuals and no one individual is allowed to exercise his rights at the expense of others.[1]

Life is the very first of these rights, the *a priori* and the *sine qua non* condition for the exercise of all the other rights. That is why democratic regimes were founded — first and foremost to protect citizens from arbitrary executions, from the terrorism of despots and their police. The promotion of other values, of other freedoms, of other goods *for all* flows from this choice of radical respect.

Contrary to what some people would have us believe, the abortion debate is not a question of "opposing views," or of "opinions" that are more or less divergent, among which the "majority" is called upon to decide. This debate calls into question what, by definition, is, or rather used to be, the object of unanimous consensus of democratic societies: the unconditional respect for others.

Although they are not always clearly aware of the thought patterns they follow, what some people fundamentally contest in the abortion debates is the very idea of universality. As we shall observe, this denial is amplified today in the debates about the new biotechnologies. Yet this idea of universality, the concrete meaning and implications of which we just discussed, is central to all democratic thought and to every democratic regime. What people are in the process of enthroning is the "static morals" characteristic of "closed societies."[2] These are morals reflecting specific interests that vary according to the convenience of those who produce them.

Of course, we cannot but observe the plurality of morals. Even Stalin and Hitler had their own morality, and it was very different from that, for example, of Gandhi or Martin Luther King. Moreover, within one and the same moral current there is room for a real pluralism. However, it is of the essence of democracy not to refer to *just any kind* of anthropology, but to take root in a minimal ethic in terms of which all men have the same dignity. Now once this idea is destroyed as the result of some particularizing regression, law and right and thus power in general — the judiciary in particular — cease to be at the service of all. It is on that point, among others, that the Marxist criticism of the liberal bourgeois State was brought to bear.

3. DENATURED DEMOCRACY

To make human life respected in democracy is not to make one "opinion" prevail over others. It is to safeguard the very possibility of any discussion about liberty, participation, equality, etc. — in short, it is to protect democracy itself.

And so, to "legalize" or "liberalize" abortion is not, despite appearances, to resolve a limited problem; it is literally to pervert the very nature of democratic society.[3] From the moment that those who orient (legislative power), control (judiciary power) or exercise (executive power) government conduct themselves as "the powerful," from the very moment the state reserves for itself the right to decide, through its institutional organs, which human being has the right to protection and respect and which human being does not, it ceases to be a democratic State because it negates the fundamental reason for which it was instituted: the defense of *every* human being's right to life. The power such a State exercises becomes arbitrary when it authorizes certain citizens to execute their *own* equals with impunity, without even offering them the possibility of being heard.

In this way, the State ceases to recognize the subjects of rights; it appropriates the definition of who is or who is not the subject of rights. The State concedes or grants rights to those it wishes to consider as subjects. Now if the State arrogates to itself an exorbitant privilege regarding the unborn infant, nothing will prevent it from going beyond that to seize the right of life and death over this or that category of the sick, the abnormal, the aged, or even over political deviants.

That is why the expression "to decriminalize abortion" is very revealing: it implicitly attributes the privilege and the power to adjust the boundary between good and evil, between what is just and unjust, to the preference of the State and the "powerful" who control its mechanisms. "What is useful to me becomes just." Yet who cannot see that the divinization of the State leads to the identification of the legal with the legitimate as well as the reduction of the person to the citizen?

One formula sums up the danger of this debate: *The liberalization of abortion laws puts into motion a political process in which the democratic State imperceptibly becomes transformed into a totalitarian State.*

4. CAESAR'S VALETS

Every arbitrary regime needs devoted personnel who will enforce the norms it establishes. Contemporary history abounds in examples that depict the capitulations and compromises acceded to especially by intellectuals. Liberalization of abortion requires a great deal of complicity: the complicity of moralists, including Christian ones, who strive to demonstrate that only the wanted child has a right to live; the complicity of psychologists who for the sake of the cause have invented a "booby-trap" distinction between the human being and the humanized being; the complicity of journalists who pretend to show that a child must be balanced against expenditure; the complicity of demographers for whom the key to development as well as to affluence is found in the fight against "human pollution"; the complicity of the legislator who makes out as though it is enough to decree that abortion is no longer a crime to make it cease being a crime; the complicity of neomalthusian ideologists who give to the woman the right of life and death over the child she bears; the complicity of the political leaders of the great world empires who want to see the population in Western Europe collapse and to contain the demographic expansion of the Third World in order to avoid sharing with it; the complicity of experts who pretend that, "science being innocent," whatever is technically possible to do is morally justified; and finally the complicity, above all, of some physicians who are among the first to be implicated in these fundamental problems. . .

5. SHEPHERDS OF LIFE AND FREEDOM

Since doctors are not only expected to speak about abortion but are required to perform it, their responsibility in this area is particularly heavy and it is important to emphasize it. By nature as well as by tradition, medicine is at the service of the patient, of his physical health and thus of the well-being of his whole person.[4] The practitioner can be faithful or not to this mission.

The example of Nazi doctors, gulag psychiatrists, and pharmacologists of "clean" torture suffices to show how far doctors who treat their patients in the interests of a third party can go. Our concern as regards these facts is reinforced by evidence that, in the very near future, the state will increasingly call upon doctors to strengthen its powers thanks to the techniques of biological engineering.

On the other hand, doctors who refuse to betray their profession appear as a real bulwark against totalitarianism. But for this bulwark to be effective, it is still necessary for medical professionals to begin to refuse *en bloc* any action against unconditional respect for human life and to denounce all manipulation as ethically indefensible. People in medical professions should repudiate all of this absolutely, instead of letting themselves concede bit by bit what they would reject globally

Once on the slippery slope, it is very difficult to stop. Wasn't Dr. Alan Guttmacher, pro-abortion leader of the Planned Parenthood Federation, also a member of the board of directors of the Euthanasia Society of America?[5] Did not a senior French magistrate recently denounce the systematic elimination, with the help of pharmaceutical formulas, of seriously ill but not bed-ridden people?[6] It seems that from now on one can dare to use even the pretext of a weak or incurable condition or a state of senility or feebleness in order to eliminate the "troublesome".

Going beyond what manipulates information and subjugates the will in this debate, the only questions that matter are simple. Yes or no: should action towards a human being — no matter how small or impaired he or she may be — be conditioned by the interests of another more powerful one? Yes or no: can the freedom of some be bought with the destruction of another's?

Thus the liberalization of abortion definitely involves fundamental philosophical questions: *either* I am the measure of the other, and this measure is some pressure group or race or party or State; *or* I welcome the other for what he really is and I allow myself to be challenged by what his existence means to me.

This debate confronts doctors with the most profound meaning of their actions: they are at the service of human life, a human life of which we are not the sovereign masters, a human life of which we have all received a share.

The reflections presented here direct us, of course, to remember the *ethical* reference point of medical activity. But above all they lead to emphasis on a seldom explored aspect of this activity, namely, that the practice of medicine brings with it more and more *political* implications and that it would be irresponsible to ignore them. Today's doctor is a shepherd of *liberty* as well as one of *life*.

6. SOCIAL TRANSCENDENCE?

As we have emphasized, the stake in these debates about human life from its beginning to its end is nothing less than democracy in its specific nature.

Such is the fragility of this type of societies that they can enact laws for themselves that in fact undermine them completely. We have seen democratic regimes that enacted racist legislation; others that made the State sacred; still others have curiously enthroned a dictator. It will soon be clear that liberalizing abortion in democratic regimes is *crossing a threshold* in many ways comparable to that crossed by "democracies" that bloodied themselves via torture or segregation.

Hence, the liberalization of abortion raises a basic political problem. Western democratic societies have remained watchful for excesses on the part of individuals and groups. These societies developed with reference to a certain philosophy of man and hence to a certain ethic; throughout the history of the West this double reference has been the source of opposition to all forms of slavery and oppression.

The most determined partisans of abortion make no bones about it. For Dr. Pierre Simon the liberalization of abortion is but a step along the long and luminous march that must perforce lead to a *new* morality, a *new* kind of politics, a *new* education, a *new* transcendence — "social transcendence."[7] It is not necessary to reflect further or observe minutely to realize that the "transcendence" of society becomes concrete only in that of the State, and that the "transcendence" of the State necessarily means the despotism of the powerful. . .

An exhaustive debate on abortion, which we will have to undertake sooner or later, will have to weigh stakes that go well beyond matters of the individual and the limits of a nation.[8] In the discussion of this difficult problem, Western countries should remember with equal fervor the price they were required to pay for their liberty. If only they would not listen to sly and dishonest intellectuals, not forget that the solutions they enact guide those who observe them and affect their credibility in the world. If only all men of good will would bear in mind that there is no such thing as a "little" murder. It is an elementary truth that human life can be neither dissected or divided. One must be either for or against. There is absolutely no room for the equivocal *yes, but. . .*

Endnotes for Chapter I:

[1] We owe to Maurice Torelli a work entitled *Le médecin et les droits de l'homme* (Paris: Berger-Levrault, 1983). See especially "From the right to life to the right to death," p. 194-217.

[2] Cf. Bergson, *Les deux sources de la morale et de la religion* (Paris: Presses Universitaires de France, 1959), e.g.: 999, 1002,1201 ff, etc., which correspond to pp. 25, 28, 283 ff of the old editions.

[3] Our book, *Démocratie et liberation chrétienne* (Paris: Lethielleux, 1986) is mostly devoted to the problem we are touching on here. We have also examined these problems in *L'enjeu politique de l'avortement* (Paris, Ed. de l'OEIL, 1991)

[4] On the relationships between medicine and morality, see Claude Bruaire, *Une éthique pour la médecine. De la responsabilité medicale à l'obligation morale* (Paris: Fayard, 1978). Contributions of unequal value can also be found in Warren T. Reich (ed.), *Encyclopedia of Bioethics*, 4 vols. (New York: The Free Press, 1982).

[5] See also Léon Schwarzenberg, *Requiem pour la vie* (Paris: Le Pre aux Clercs, 1985). See also this doctor's statement in his interview with Pierre Demeron and published under the title "La vérité est toujours bonne à dire," in *Marie-Claire*, Oct. 1985, 26, 29 f., 32.

[6] We refer to the conference given in Paris on January 24, 1981, by Claude Jacquinot for the National Congress of the Association "Laissez-les vivre."

[7] The expression appears in Pierre Simon, *De la vie avant toute chose* (Paris: Mazarine, 1979) 240.

[8] In fact, this new debate has already begun. See, for example, J. H. Soutoul and collaborators, *Conséquences d'une loi après 600 jours d'avortements légaux* (Paris: La Table Ronde, 1977); Joël-Benoît d'Onorio, "Loi Veil: réflexions sur un premier bilan," in *La semaine juridique* 60:23 (June 4, 1986) I: *Doctrine*, 3246 (bibliography); Henri Guitton et al, *L'avortement. Mille médecins témoignent*, Academy of Education and Social Studies (Paris: Ed. de Fleurus, 1986).

chapter II

ETHICS AND BIOPOLITICS

Once stripped of its presuppositions, the debate over laws liberalizing abortion reveals how closely intertwined are political power and power over life. Nowadays what affords power over life is a collection of knowledge and techniques heretofore absolutely unimaginable. In this the "art" of the abortionist can be an eminently suggestive, though limited, example.

Whatever relates to human life, its maintenance and development, is of interest to politics. We already know this to be the case with medicine, biology and demography, as well as with the sciences sometimes grouped under the generic title "biotics." The term "biopolitics" describe s the exploitation of the resources of these sciences with a view to appropriating and/or exercising political power. International organizations, governments, private groups, the experts themselves can all be tempted to use the various disciplines that form biotics for political ends. This kind of manipulation, however, poses grave and complex problems in the realm of social morality. The tenacious effort on the part of some to decriminalize abortion gives but a glimpse of the presence of a looming iceberg. It is the base of this iceberg that we ought now to explore.

1. SCIENCE AND POLITICS

For a long time, the relationship between science and political power has been close yet fairly unclear.[1] By science, we understand here an organic ensemble of knowledge concerning an area of natural reality. Thus biology is the knowledge regarding the domain of life; medicine is the area of knowledge that deals with health, how to preserve and recover it; and demography is an area of knowledge dealing with population, its condition and evolution.

The effectiveness of science includes the unheard of capacity to intervene in nature, man and society. To employ this capacity in the exercise of government is fascinating to politicians. From this point of view, politicians are in the power of scientists, or at least dependent on them. On the other hand, scientists find themselves dependent on politicians to the extent that they cannot define their projects or conduct their research without governmental support.

This odd relationship between science and politics manifests itself in various ways. It can be observed in the interplay between political power on one hand and, on the other, the economy, finance, physics, applied sciences and military engineering.[2] Whoever controls the economy, monetary affairs or army is able to make his own interests predominate over those of others. This kind of relationship has often led to *reductionist theories* of political power, which in a democratic society involve reciprocity, recognition and participation. By *"reductionist theories"* we mean that political power is emptied of its specifics, that it is reduced to or identified with something other than itself. It is identified instead according to the circumstances, with industrial capital, financial capital, the means of production, or the armed forces.

These last are, each in its own way, producers of power. Those who control them have available a *de facto* power, an ability to influence the behavior of men without the latter having any say in the domination exercised over them. The legitimacy of this de facto power is questionable in its very principle. It is nothing but pseudo-authority, nothing but might; and might thus understood entails for those who exercise it the possibility of exacting submission. If I am stronger economically or militarily, I can require submission from those who are weaker. I can exercise control over them , leaving them powerless. This intimidation can go to the extreme of radical violence, that is, all the way to death.

It was early in the history of political thought and activity that political authority was reduced to the element of might. We can even say that political power — in its fully human conception — was slowly disengaged from critical thought concerning might. For some Sophists, power was linked to force — as was right. The se Sophists simply mirrored the almost commonplace thinking of their era. La Fontaine, the 17th century fable writer, echoed the thinking of the Sophists when he tried to demonstrate that "The reason of the strongest is always better."

Basing "power" on force necessarily bears a corresponding conception of justice: if I am stronger, I am able to define right and will do so to suit my own interests. Right becomes utilitarian and advantageous only to some. What I identify as just will be just, and this definition will consider only my own well-being. I will perceive as a threat anything that risks calling my superiority — which my strength insures — into question. For reasons of utility and mutual interest, I can get along with others who are as strong as I. But I have no obligation regarding those who are weaker, nor will they enjoy any right insofar as I am concerned.

Today the problem is, above all, the relationship between political power and biomedical sciences.[3] More than fifty years ago, some physicists — and not the least learned ones — put the resources of nuclear physics at the disposal of the heads of States. Presently, both biotics as well as demography offer their resources to the world's masters.[4] Furthermore, certain experts in these disciplines are inclined to take advantage of the ever-increasing power in their hands in order to intervene in the governing of men. In short, in political life, those who control the science of life (biologists, physicians, demographers) tend to intervene directly as well as indirectly.

2. SOME COMPLEX MORAL PROBLEMS

This new situation poses complex problems that require the attention of moralists. What are the concrete signs of this might? Who are its victims? Who produces these signs? Who profits from them? What are their aims? What ideology do they propose as justification for their actions? Above all, what are the moral problems that arise from these practices? These and other questions stand compellingly on the horizon of ethical reflection. Imperialism is no longer limited to military or economic muscle. Now it also avails itself of the support of new scientific practices and discoveries, and those presented by the life-sciences rank first.[5]

To examine some of the unprecedented moral challenges hurled at the men of our time will prepare us to analyze the techniques of in vitro fertilization and embryo transfer. The implications of the success of these procedures allow us to disentangle in a clear way the moral problems posed by modern biomedical sciences.[6]

From among the many new practices, let us limit ourselves to the following:

—Interference with the *sperm*. Sperm can be preserved indefinitely, which permits its use after the death of the donor.

Moreover, in the case of sterility in the husband, recourse to a third party as donor is no longer at all exceptional.

—While the *ova* cannot be preserved at this time, the handling of embryos as if they were inventory in a "warehouse" in preparation for implantation in the uterus of the mother or of a "surrogate" is becoming a frequent practice.

—*Fetuses* (embryos of three or more months) are frequently used as material for laboratories and/or for use by the cosmetic industry.

—We must also make mention of *prenatal control* methods. The elimination of embryos or fetuses that certain tests indicate are more or less probable carriers of congenital defects is increasingly recommended and practiced.

—Judging from the evidence, the pinnacle of this technological mastery over the embryo is *in vitro fertilization*. This is one of the most commented upon procedures today. In vitro fertilization can be accomplished with several different procedures.

By way of example, let us consider a very simple case in which one would have recourse to in vitro fertilization: obstruction of the fallopian tubes. After appropriate hormonal treatment, under anesthesia, ripe ova can be removed from a woman's ovary and then can be fertilized in vitro with the sperm of her husband. One of these fertilized ova is subsequently reimplanted in the woman's uterus, who brings the pregnancy to term.

Of course, it remains to be seen what will happen to the fertilized ova that were not used. Assurances are given that they will be frozen, and in case the first attempt at implantation does not succeed, they will be used in a future attempt. Immediately, however, questions arise. What is to happen to the fertilized ova that will not be implanted? What is their destiny? Who will have control over them and why?

The problem is not purely theoretical, as can be seen in the following case. Antonio Hernandez , a Chilean, had made his fortune in copper. He had a son, Juan, from a first marriage. He took Conchita as his second wife. He wanted children, but since they came up against some problem that was unsolvable in Chile, they bought a ticket for Melbourne. The doctors removed some ova from Conchita; a carefully selected sperm donor was summoned with all due discretion, and in vitro fertilization took place. The successfully created embryos were frozen. But then before the implantation procedure could be arranged, Antonio and Conchita died in an airplane accident. Questions presented themselves without delay. What was to be done with the frozen embryos? Let them die? Implant them? In whom? What would be the rights of the "surrogate" over the child? And then who would inherit Antonio's fortune? Juan? The child or children born of surrogacy?

The problem became even more complex, since a medical professional's indiscretion, perhaps deliberate, revealed that Antonio was not the biological father of the embryos. Who was to decide, and by what right, the future of the frozen embryos? Juan? A judge? The "State"? The doctors? In this case, money forced these pointed questions into the limelight, questions that otherwise would have been buried in thick silence.

These questions are truly of capital importance, for , biologically speaking, it is an established fact that the fertilized egg is an individual in the precise sense of this term. The combination of the gametes — each already a bearer of an original rearrangement of the genetic patrimony of the parents (the result of meiosis) — is the point of departure for a new biological individual. It is from this moment on that the zygote has a genetic identity card unlike any other. Individuation, then, occurs prior to nesting, which will allow the fertilized egg to attach to the uterine wall and there find all it needs to develop.[7] The fact of individuation is solidly established at the scientific level, so much so that it is as indisputable as the circulation of blood. There simply is no other biological criterion that allows us to fix the beginning of a human being at another moment.

Recalling another, not in the least hypothetical, case will allow us to understand better the serious problems that in vitro fertilization can pose in short order. Today it is possible to call a human being into existence who will not come to know either his father, or mother, or even his surrogate. An ova aspirated from donor A can be fertilized in vitro by the sperm of donor B and then be implanted in the uterus of surrogate C. A child born under these conditions might not know the identity of A, B or C. He would be, from the very beginning, a human being *deprived of all kinship*. Now, the most spontaneous and elementary way to ascertain anyone's identity is to determine his filiation. This is even the source of many patronymics: Janssens, Johnson, etc. But in this case, the human being would be an individual without reference to anybody. He would be divested at the outset of all interpersonal relationships. Thrust into existence, absolutely alone and without protection, he would be exposed to the denial of legal recognition; no one would have to answer for him, and he himself would be responsible to no one. He would be at the mercy of the technician who brought him into existence, at the mercy of that technician's boss.

3. ARE WE ALL WARDS OF THE REPUBLIC?

One can forecast the tangle of problems these procedures will give rise to hereafter. If a State, a party, an "elite" (racial, scientific, etc.), or whatever kind of "nomenklatura" were to appropriate control over the production of human beings, it would exercise power over subjects ignorant of their origin. Moreover, the absence of the interpersonal relationships of paternity and maternity with the biological rooting that these entail, calls into question the love life of man and woman and the sexual involvement that *it* implies.

The dream of certain people becomes a reality: individuals are sent back to their solitary pleasure, and "society mediated by the doctor" liberates them of all responsibility toward partners and descendants.[8] This trend was pointed out by Simone Veil, who brought about the legalization of abortion in France: "One observes a certain tendency toward ever greater privatization of sexuality, and reproduction considered more and more as the affair of the couple and theirs alone, while the consequences (that is to say, the children) are increasingly collectivized."[9] We are at the brink of nationalized human reproduction. In the end, the fracture of these interpersonal, loving, parental, fraternal relationships will impair and destroy the whole fabric of the family.[10] For this to come about it is necessary to attack the weakest link in the chain: the unborn child. How can we doubt that certain brotherhoods, mentioned nonchalantly by Dr. Pierre Simon and abundantly represented in all sorts of organizations, have not made this project foremost in their program?

Thus for the first time in history, biological resources offer to totalitarian utopians the technical possibility of realizing their dream. Plato, Aristotle and Campanella were able to dream of a shining city that would control the quantity and quality of children. Today, the "total mastery over fertility" is offered as one *possibility*. Authoritarian States or powerful groups will soon have to do nothing more than hold out their hand in order to appropriate and control the production of fatherless and motherless beings — wards of their total devotion.

Yet that is not all! These new slaves will have to conform as nearly as possible to a predetermined model. Malthus' and Darwin's much-extolled principle of *natural* selection cannot be allowed to operate. Following the lines of Galton, an *artificial* selection will have to be instituted, a eugenics program modeled after the available techniques. The State , a similar institution, or a private group will define the standards, the "norms," that the production of human individuals must follow, taking into account the qualitative and quantitative demands imperiously required by the projected society it wishes to establish.[11] In short, politics will be reduced to managing human cattle.

Of course, there is no question of stopping on our way down this beautiful road. The holders of power will have to provide for the *education* of the individuals they will have admitted into existence. A great, unrivaled and evidently very secular educational system will do the job!

The State — and more precisely the particular group that will "occupy" it — will thus be the new Providence. After deciding through the mediation of doctors and biologists who will live and who must die, who can or must donate their germinal cells, the management of this "material" will be foremost amongst their objectives.

The blessed chosen ones and their progeny will then be entirely in their care: all "wards of the Republic." This was altogether foreseen by the Marquis de Sade: "In France, where the population is too numerous,. . .it will be necessary to fix the numbers of children, to drown the rest without pity. . .The government, master now of all these children and of their number, would necessarily have as many defenders as it would have raised."[12]

A eugenics project that was almost as ambitious, we might recall, was part of *Mein Kampf*.[13] It was there that arose the idea of permitting, even of obliging in the name of patriotism, the procreation of individuals according to the "norms" of a racist ideology. It was there that its negative corollary, the idea of forbidding and even of advancing the hopelessness of reproduction for those individuals deemed too divergent from the "norms" in question[14] also saw the light of day. However, as the manipulations have become much more refined and the techniques more effective, the "norm" can be defined with greater precision and applied with the pitiless rigor that efficiency requires.

4. TOWARDS THE INSTITUTIONAL IMBROGLIO

If these new practices bear direct implications for education, they have implications on the legal level as well.

In reality, *right* organizes the connections between individuals, the relationships between persons. More precisely, all the juridical institutions of our democratic societies are founded on the protection of the individual human being and his relationships to others. Now if right does not take into account the individual character, the genetic singularity of the fertilized cell, we run straight into contradictions and inconsistencies that add to those raised above regarding abortion.

Since January 17, 1975, French legislation has shown a charming fearlessness in these matters. Article 1 of the Veil law says: "The law guarantees respect for every human being from the beginning of life." The same article continues with an insolence that leaves a logician breathless: "This principle may not be infringed upon except in the case of necessity according to the conditions defined by the present law." We know in practice that this second part of the article permits legal killing all the way up to the third month of gestation, if it is expedient for a mother oppressed too often by her partner or the hypocrisy of a sensual society. More recently, a regulation acknowledged that the embryo is a human person and codified the use of a dead fetuses (!) — without inquiring too much into the causes and circumstances of these deaths![15]

Perhaps the next demand will be for a law that protects embryos that another law has allowed to be killed after three months. Someone is dreaming. . .

Such artistry in legal dispositions is just the thing to distract from the truth with many contradictions. It distracts all the more insofar as it insinuates that inconsistency in the texts is merely a passing phase in a calculated strategy. The articles that contradict the foundations of our current civil codes *in practice* could very well constitute the first attempts at a new code, built on the same bases as these articles. Our entire body of laws until now has bespoken a comprehensive concept of the person that declares that every living human being is considered a person and must be treated as such. We must now positively fear that, after being twisted and placed in opposition to itself, the notion of personhood will in the end be curtailed. To reduce the meaning of the person is to throw out of its embrace a whole series of subjects (embryos, the mentally ill, the aged) and to declare them nonpersons, a prerequisite for getting rid of them with impunity or for using them for profit. The code will be whittled down to the point of accommodating a selective definition of person.

From the moment that right takes leave of individuation — this most basic of biological givens — everything without exception is permissible in the name of fact. The gurus consider "it" to be a mere "chemical product," a "mass of cells," therefore "it" is neither individual nor person. And the "moralists" nod their assent.

These procedures, once habitual, will serve as the precedent or legal basis for right. Ova are fertilized in vitro *today*; embryos are killed or let to die *today*. Thus these procedures *are* done; then they *may* be done; then they even *should* be done. The law recognizes them, authorizes them; soon perhaps the law will prescribe them. They will sever all reference to morality; worse, they will be identified *as* morality. Right will soon be purely positive, in the sense that it will no longer be rooted in solidly based principles. We will be in the embrace of absolute relativism, *except for one point*: right and morality, henceforth debauched, will bless only what is *done*, only what the *strongest already do*.

The discussion on abortion has highlighted the double tendency of becoming less and less interested in the child as individual with this disinterest working in favor of the adult as individual. Yet a new difficulty ensues: one loses interest in the individual in general, and *this* disinterest works to the profit of the minority that directly or indirectly controls access to medical technology. Thus this entire line of thought and practice directly and radically contests the very *universal* weight of the *Declaration of the Rights of Man* (1948).

Thus the legal difficulties result in inextricable *political* difficulties. To underline the genetic singularity of the human individual from the moment of conception enriches the idea of *universality* with an original and irreducible foundation, the very universality that is one of the main supports of democracy.[16] In a democracy, there is no favoritism: all are equal and free, independent of their physical, intellectual, moral, religious, etc. differences. Every institutional apparatus, legal as well as political, aims to protect this singularity and to assist individuals in their personal realization. This fulfillment will be accomplished through recognition, reciprocity and participation — in short, within the framework of a relational fabric as rich as it is complex, and watched over by the law.

No sooner is the human individual's genetic singularity from conception established than this splendid gain is sidestepped by barely disguised cliques who base their ascendancy on the for-profit exploitation of new biological and medical procedures. In rejecting the premise of the human individual as such, every decision to follow will be of a discriminatory and arbitrary character. These decisions will emanate from the mere choice of those who can make their will dominant. Here again we see full *positivism*.

However, this same positivism, extraordinarily convenient in the designs of the mighty, turns against those who have just found it to their advantage. For, having set aside the essential biological reference, the need to furnish a new biological definition of the human individual will be required all the same. We see looming, ever multiplied in gravity and number, the difficulties that abortion engenders. What will the basis for the definition of the human individual now be? Where shall we place the cut-off point? Will we say, and on what basis, that individuation takes place at the time of implantation, at six weeks, at three months, or at birth? Anything and everything can be affirmed, if we turn our backs on the most solid and least contested gains of contemporary biology. Anything and everything: this means that whatever we have yet to discover about the fundamental scientific reality of individuation from the moment of conception will be deemed an expression of obscurantism and prejudice. Furthermore, what is declared human here could be declared a mass of cells in the neighboring region or some other country. Here the human person finds protection, there arbitrariness.

As if these discrepancies were not enough, they become even more complicated in view of the possibilities opened up by cloning. Both abortion and in vitro fertilization force us to see the peril in definitions of the human being patterned after particular convenience and interests. Although the role of achievements is to lend flesh and blood to the dreams and images of some, the possibilities in cloning would aggravate an already extremely complex situation: In the first two cases mentioned, it is only (if we dare say it thus) a matter of interfering with "ordinary" human individuals; in the matter of cloning, however, we have the explicit will to produce an indefinite number of identical individuals, chosen according to well specified criteria. What sense can it possibly make to speak of identical human beings? If such projects are attained by necessity on the basis of human genetic material, can we still even speak of "human beings"? How will we decide who these are?

5. A NEW CHALLENGE FOR SOCIAL ETHICS

From what we have seen, biomedical achievements — all heavy with educational, legal and political implications — challenge moralists directly; they must, more than ever, be attentive to the signs of the times.

In our first chapter, abortion and its liberalization were shown to be a problem of social and political morality.[17] The same is true concerning biomedical technology, particularly in vitro fertilization and genetic manipulation.

In social ethics, the moralist certainly has reason to be concerned about peace and its conditions. But this concern does not justify falling back in a war. The weapons that were available to the superpowers in the "old" confrontation between East and West applied mastery over atoms and space primarily. However, when it comes to the confrontation between North and South, directors of public and private international organizations have begun to exploit biomedical resources more and more. The rationale invoked by these organizations varies: the right of a couple to children, promotion of the feminist cause, "euconception," socioeconomic considerations, etc. In short, the complete Malthusian and NeoMalthusian tradition is put to use. Yet among the justifications, one stands out with increasing clarity: many believe that the time has passed when it was necessary to resist the push of the communist world because of East-West antagonism. Hereafter what is necessary is to contain the demographic expansion of the Third World.

The Second World Conference on Population that took place in Mexico from August 6-13, 1984, revealed that at the end of this century the population of the globe will have gone from 4.8 billion to 6.2 billion inhabitants. Of these 6.2 billion, 80% will be living in the Third World, and 50% of them will be less than 25 years old. The whole arsenal of biomedical resources must be mobilized to contain this rise in young people. This plan is recommended and financed by International Planned Parenthood, other similar organizations, and the World Bank to cite just a few.[18] But we must not forget that the same arsenal is employed albeit in a less sophisticated way in China, where the government imposes a clearly coercive plan for births.

While keeping in view the ethical questions raised by the arms race, the moralist must from now on anticipate the coming war — the one which is, in fact, already in full swing both within nations and on an international plane. This war is the one that mobilizes the biomedical arsenal to defend the interests of the strongest to the detriment of the weakest.

The same thing goes for morality as for politics. It is the duty of the moralist to think out all the consequences of what contemporary biology teaches us about fertilization and individuation. For the moralist to fix the threshold of humanization elsewhere is nothing short of engaging in fantasy. This given, to which we must always return, also clarifies the role of parents, the meaning of sexuality and of human fecundity. Neither parent gives to him- or herself the ability to transmit life. More precisely, neither of the two is totally master of the genetic capital he or she possesses, a capital that is brought to its full potential at the time of fertilization. Parents have received this capacity; they receive it at the moment they receive life; they are the carriers. Human sexuality and fecundity, then, involve managing and employing the ability to transmit human life, with its prodigious potential for originality, its potential for genetic individuality, that blossoms first and foremost within the family in the form of personality.[19]

The debate on abortion has shown that when moralists ignore elementary biological data, they embark on a route that, from implantation to birth, opens the way to definitions of man according to a variable geometry. In the era of in vitro fertilization , moralists who accept definitions à la carte cannot but encourage unscrupulous governments and groups to exploit the new biotechniques to their own profit with the aim of establishing a new kind of society. Furthermore, they impel them to improve on techniques that are yet to be more effective than those available today.

6. FROM STRUCTURAL VIOLENCE TO GENETIC VIOLENCE

Whatever happens in the secrecy of certain antiseptic rooms goes well beyond the sphere of private morality. The practices of sterilization and abortion, as we have seen, correlate to the artificial selection extolled by Galton[20] and combine with the structural violence described by Galtung.[21] The latter plays the role of an active restraint in the process of natural selection proposed by Malthus.[22] Yet a new stage is on the verge of being reached: those in political power, in order to add to it, can avail themselves of two new possibilities, namely, surgical violence and genetic violence. The first is manifested in abortions and sterilizations; the second affects heredity, in view, they hope, of fabricating human beings produced by the genius of amoral technicians.

The natural selection described by Malthus and the artificial selection recommended by Galton have doubtlessly suggested to politicians a means to extend their de facto power. This extension of power is product of the effort to contain population, an effort that is natural and admissible in Malthus, or artificial and provoked in Galton. The expansion of power available to politicians is no longer of a quantitative nature; now it also stems from the new possibilities for interference in the very quality of life. The moment life is reduced to "material to manage" and its management is entrusted to pure technicians, everything, or almost everything, becomes possible, and what is possible becomes desirable. It will be a question of managing human cattle, to plan their reproduction, to settle on quotas of the more suitable and the less suitable.

We can thus catch a glimpse of the ultimate stakes of these research and experimental programs. It is, first of all, a matter of controlling the human being from the *beginning* of his or her existence. "Ordinary" parents are demoted. The only function still conceded to them — only because it is impossible to do otherwise — consists in beseeching them to furnish, after "rigorous selection," the cells that the manipulators will appropriate. The genetic capital of humanity in this way risks being stolen from those who are its bearers. They will be dispossessed by the scientist, the State, the institution, the firm, the insurance company, etc.

It has become a question of controlling the *originality* of individuals. The traditional methods of transmission of life contained a vast reserve of incertitude and the unforeseen. With these, nothing allowed doctors to forecast the chromosomal makeup of an *individual*. It was precisely this singularity of each person that made up the richness of humanity. However, from now on it will be necessary to overcome the uncertainty, to leave nothing to chance any longer. Furthermore, cloning is also bringing to light a new era that will see identical individuals flourish. It is ultimately the originality of the species that is threatened. We have always been familiar with the hybridization of races; we now contemplate the hybridization of species, at great expense. What kind of a monstrous being will result from such crossbreeding?

These assaults made on the *biological* originality of individuals and the species are all the more disturbing as they have been preceded, as we know, by many assaults made on the *psychological* originality of men by the repressive use of psychiatry. Indoctrination and ideological subjugation pave the way for the creation of biological uniformity and vice versa.

Finally, the life that they strive to control in its origin and quality, must equally be controlled in its *duration*. Euthanasia will make complete the seizure of an individual's entire biological process by vowing him or her to death.

The ideology inspiring these biopolitical projects appears to call for a reformulation of the theory of class struggle, where the struggle is no longer expressed in economic terms but genetic ones. Here again we encounter scientific tradition: once again it will spark a concept of justice based on nature's determinism, particularly on the relationship between forces. Previously, the economically strongest were right, at least for a while; now, the genetically strongest have law on their side.

If nature commands, or a group pretends that nature commands, that there are some men carrying "good genes" and others who carry "bad genes," justice and right will be adjusted according to the inclination of the genetic category, the genetic class, to which individuals presumedly will belong.

Endnotes for Chapter II:

[1] Cf. J. J. Salomon, *Science et politique* (Paris: Seuil, 1970). See particularly *Biology as a Social Weapon*, Ann Arbor, MI.: Ann Arbor Science for the People Editorial Collective (Minneapolis: Burgess, 1977).

[2] For an analysis of the modern State's tendency to interfere, see Jean Meyer, *Le poids de l'Etat* (Paris: Presses Universitaires de France, 1983).

[3] The problem was studied by Pierre Thuillier in *Les biologistes vont-ils prendre le pouvoir? La sociobiologie en question, 1. Le contexte et l'enjeu* (Brussels: Ed. Complexe, Coll. de la science, 1981). Let us cite at least one work representative of a sociobiological current: Charles Lumsden and Edward Wilson, *Le feu du Prométhée. Réflexions sur l'origine de l'esprit* (Paris: Mazarine, 1984). I have analyzed a case of *military* technocracy in *Destin du Brésil* (Gembloux: Duculot, 1973).

[4] Regarding the subjection of science to a political ideology, see, for example: Jean Paul II, "Rencontre avec des hommes de science et des étudiants,"Cologne, Nov. 15, 1980, in *Documentation catholique* no. 1798 (Dec. 21, 1980) 1130; "Libérez la science de la violence des riches et des puissants. Discours à l'Assemblée plénière de l'"Académie pontificale des sciences," *ibid.* no. 1864 (Dec. 18, 1983) 1133-1136.

[5] Prof. Jean Dausset, Nobel Prize winner, shared his puzzlement on this in in an article entitled "Les apprentis sorciers," *Le Monde,* Dec. 16, 1984.

[6] Popularizations of the problems here mentioned can be found in the special issue of *La Recherche* devoted to "La génétique et l'hérédité," no. 155 (May 1984); "Génétique: les sorciers de la vie," in *L'Express* (August 31, 1984) 16-24; "The New Origins of Life," in Time no. 37 (Sept. 19, 1984) 34-43.

[7] A reference work was just given me by Philippe Caspar, doctor of medicine and philosophy, *L'individuation des êtres: Aristotle, Liebniz et l'immunologie contemporaine* (Paris-Namur: Lethielleux, 2985). See the two exposés published by the same author under the title "Les fondements de l'individuality biologique,"in *Communio* IX (Nov-Dec. 1984) 80-91; "Pour un principe d'individuation des êtres vivants" in *Revue des Questions Scientifiques* 155 (4) (1984) 423-434.

[8] One of the most revealing books on the scientistic and Masonic inspiration behind certain contemporary biocracy is that of Dr. Pierre Simon, *De la vie avant toute chose* (Paris: Mazarine, 1979) 222.

[9] (Sic) Simone Veil, "Exposé," published in Mexico 1977: *International Population Conference Proceedings* (Liege: Union internationale pour l'etude scientifique, 1977) 598.

[10] Cf. P. Simon, *ibid.* 96, 22 and *passim.*

[11] This point figures in the States' program in Singapore and appears clearly in the People's Republic of China. Lee Kuan Yew developed these topics in his speech at the national day cultural show and rally held at the national theater on Aug. 14, 1983. Mr. Lee Kuan Yew's eugenic theses and practices allege scientific foundations and rest on an ideology close to that by Hitler. See the volume, *Designer Genes: I. Q., Ideology and Biology* (Selangor, Malaysia: Institute for Social Analysis, 1984). Note that the majority of the collaborators in this work (among them Noam Chomsky) are Anglo-Saxons. On the last page of the cover a text of Lee Kuan Yew is compared with a parallel text of Hitler in peaceful cynicism. See also Jacques Decornoy. "L'Asie du Sud-Est encrise de développement," *Le Monde* (Nov. 23, 1983).

[12] Sade, *Les prospérités du vice* (Paris, Union générale d'Editions, 1969) 55.

[13] Hitler explains these ideas *passim* and especially on pp. 398-404 of *Mein Kampf* (Paris: Nouvelles Éditions latines). All of the problems we touch upon here are also treated by Plato, notably in book 5, 458e-462a of the *Republic*. For Plato's contribution (and that of others) on the question of totalitarian machines, see Jean-Jaques Walter, *Les machines totalitaires*, (Paris: Ed. Denoël, 1982), especially ch. IX (213-238; cfr. p. 226 and 252 ff).

[14] The idea of "permission to procreate" reappeared later. It is proposed by, among others, René Dumont, *L'Utopie ou la mort* (Paird: Seuil, 1973), cf. 48-50.

[15] See in this regard *Conférence de presse* by M. Ed. Hervé, Secretary of State for Health, on the theme "Ethique et Santé," given on July 12, 1984. The text can be found in the doctoral thesis for medicine presented in 1985 to the Faculté de Médecine de Tours by Patricia Soutoul under the title *L'information médicale continue du grand public en matière de reproduction humaine*. See pp. 239-246. Furthermore, echoing the call of Prof. Jean-Louis Touraine, *Le Monde* (May 30, 1985) announced "une croisade pour les greffes des tissus foetaux." Recall in this regard that the recent evolution of jurisprudence and/or legislation concerning the removal of organs from cadavers could lead the way to abuse in the use of gametes.

[16] See in this regard our book *Démocratie et libération chrétienne* (Paris: Lethielleux, 1986) 30-44.

[17] Cf. also our work, *L'enjeu politique de l'avortement* (Paris: Ed. de l'OEIL, 1991).

[18] Skeptics can get an idea of what is going on and what is in store by checking the *Onzième rapport annuel de l'Organization mondiale de la Santé*, presenting the *Programme spécial de recherche, de développement et de formation à la recherche en reproduction humaine*, Geneva, November 1982. On the Conference in Mexico, see Pierre Chaunu, *L'Historien en cet instant* (Paris: Hachette, 1985) esp. ch XIV: "Se taire à Mexico," 254-264 and "Ce qu'ils ont tu: Le mensonge par omission," 265-285.

[19] On this matter see Marie-Odile Rethore, "Recherches génétiques et conscience chrétienne," *Amour et familie* (CLER, no. 137 (Nov. 1982) 3-14, esp. 5.

[20] Francis Galton (1822-1911) published in 1869 *Hereditary Genius. An Inquiry into its Laws and Consequences* (London: Macmillan, 1982).

[21] A brief exposé of his positions can be found in "Entretien avec Johann Galtung," *Alternatives non violentes, Dossier Désobéissance civile* no. 34 (Lyon, 1980) 66-74.

[22] Malthus (1766-1834) is the author of the famous *Essai sur le principe de population* (London: 1798). On the preventive brake, see ch. IV; on the active brake, see ch. V. "The perspective of supporting a family acts as a preventive brake on the natural increase of the population, and. . .the present poverty of certain elements of the lower classes, which denies them the possibility of providing appropriately for the care and feeding of their children, plays the role of active brake." (p. 44).

chapter III

IN VITRO FERTILIZATION: AN ATTEMPT AT SYNTHESIS

Controversy about in vitro fertilization followed the debate on abortion. Yet where passions were let loose about abortion, in vitro fertilization seemed to freeze the judgment of public opinion. From all that he reads and hears, "the man in the street" appears to remember only the extreme division among specialists and moralists. He finds himself before a vast pattern of incompatible positions that all pretend to be equally well founded. Even among Christians the predominant impression is that it is an open matter left to the unfettered judgment of each person, that it is a question where conscience has no strict norms of guidance. Some Catholic quarters go so far as to interpret the "silence" of the Magisterium[1] in this manner.

In fact, the complexity of the problem was thrown into the face of the public apparently in order to cover up not only the gravity of what is at stake but also the relative simplicity of the elements that serve as its solution.

In order to resolve a new problem, we must try to grasp it in as clear a manner as possible, taking into account each of its elements. This is what we will try to do in the present chapter. We will approach in vitro fertilization and transfer of the embryo in a series of complementary steps. First we will take a look at the nature of the embryo as well as the purpose for its manipulation. We will then inquire into the implications of these practices on the level of the family and of political society. What ideology supports them? What is the value of these procedures from an epistemological as well as medical point of view? Finally, we will explore the response they have elicited from Catholic Magisterium.

1. THE NATURE OF THE EMBRYO

A. On the strictly biological level, the fertilization of an ovum by the sperm constitutes the beginning of a new individual. This proposition is neither the expression of an opinion nor a haphazard hypothesis. It is a statement of *fact* of scientific order. From the moment of conception the new being is individualized principally by its genetic code; commanded with precision by this code, the human being will develop in a continuous fashion. This individuation occurs in every case of conception whether it is realized through "the methods of an artisan,"[2] by artificial insemination, or by in vitro fertilization.

B. Biology's recently acquired knowledge is precious to the *philosopher* particularly in the area of ontology.

1) In the light of contemporary biology, the medieval theories that tended to separate the moment of "animation" from that of "conception" are now seen to be groundless hypotheses. These theories relied on the data of Aristotelian embryology which we now know was strictly limited. Today there is no reason to deny that the human spiritual soul is created by God at the very moment of conception,[3] and if this is the case, it means that from that moment on there exists a new substance endowed with a spiritual soul, the basis of intellectual and voluntary activity. In other words, from the moment of conception the human being, with its distinctness established by biology, is a subsistent reality that fully corresponds to the definition of person provided by Boethius: *rationalis creaturae individua substantia*, the individual essence of a rational creature. The *most elementary* moral prudence, then, demands that we recognize here a human subject with rights.

Briefly put, if the act of individuation (conception) coincides with the act of personalization (animation), then the person is in act from the moment of conception.[4]

2) From the ontological point of view, rational and voluntary activity will always manifest itself even if in a progressive manner. But this is of the *accidental* order and in no way calls into question the existence of the subsistent reality itself.

3) The human person is a social being: by nature, a person is called to enter into *relationship* with other persons. But it is ridiculous to base the existence of the person on his relationships with others. Obviously, quite the opposite is true: interpersonal relationships are founded on the existence of persons capable of such relations.

Robinson Crusoe did not cease to be a person just because he found himself stranded on a desert island!

4) Now to resolve a final difficulty. We know that in order to clarify the question of in vitro fertilization, a frequent recourse is the Aristotelian doublet of act and potency: the embryo would be "human only in potency."[5] This perspective results in a confusion between the first act, entitative, and the second act, operative. From the outset the human embryo is a substance whose individuation takes place according to a specific mode of personalization. Besides being a human person in the act of existence, the embryo is also in potency to receive, thanks to its activity, accidental determinations. These latter acts, called "second" acts, in no way change the substantive reality that abides throughout any changes.

2. THE AIMS OF IN VITRO FERTILIZATION

A. In vitro fertilization and transfer of the embryo constitute *experimentation* on a human fertilized egg. First, of course, one had to begin by perfecting these procedures. Nowadays — without mentioning what has gone before — we have reached a success rate of about ten percent; put another way, according to *La Palice*, there is a ninety percent failure rate — a holocaust! Next, since the success of the procedure is so erratic, in vitro fertilization requires the production of a large number of surplus embryos. Finally, the circle is closed inasmuch as the presence of surplus embryos encourages experimentation.

The theoretical dream that looks forward to a hundred percent success rate in the more or less distant future cannot justify in any case , even in anticipation of this eventual success, the actual sacrifice of a hundred embryos, not even, to tell the truth, of a single one.

B. We can only wonder if the motivation of experimentation itself is not, for some researchers, reason enough for the procedure. Scientific and medical circles have never been asked to explain this aspect. Professor Férin, an authority if there is any in these matters, wrote plainly in 1973: "In the thinking of biologists, some of the human eggs thus obtained will be destined for sacrifice, first of all in order to perfect the method itself." There follow three other reasons "for which the biologists will practically have need to sacrifice a certain number of human eggs": to gain knowledge of the first stages of development, to attempt medication, and to judge the effectiveness of the method.[6] It could hardly be more clearly spelled out!

Thus knowledge becomes an end in itself, an absolute goal, as if the value of scientific progress were independent of its context and methods, as if it were without relation to the human beings who achieve it and those who pay the price for it.

It is sophism to claim that in the name of the legitimate quest for knowledge — even in areas such as normal birth, immunity, grafting, cancer — the scientist may do anything, including disposing of another human being's life. Like all human activity, scientific activity is subject to moral norms. No claim relative to academic freedom can take away from the unconditional respect that is due every human being. No man, no matter what his concrete condition might be, may be used as a guinea pig for scientific ends. Science is at the service of man; man is not at the service of science.

These are the limits that morality imposes on *experimentation*. To perform experiments on a human being is not admissible, for example, in medicine or surgery, except with the permission of the subject, or, put differently, only if the experimenter-"experimentee" relationship is cast within the relationship of human-to-human, only if the experimenter recognizes the subject as a human being and *treats him* or *her as such*. To forget this mandatory restriction contains the germ of perversion for medicine.

C. It makes no sense to consider the *experimental* character of in vitro fertilization as secondary to the primary *therapeutic* goal, that is, to remedy sterility.

1) This technique in no way proposes to remedy sterility but only to alleviate its consequences. The problem is not at all resolved — it is bypassed. No one is ministered to; no one is healed. Instead, very simply, a skillful maneuver is made — one that entails a perfectly well recognized danger of death for some embryonic human beings.

2) It is beyond the scope of our project to give an even cursory picture of the complex phenomenon we call human sterility. The cure for this disorder, while recognized and studied since ancient times — particularly by Hippocratic doctors and great biologists such as Aristotle — has never ceased to mobilize the efforts of the medical corps. Recall, for example, the remarkable modern gains made in the knowledge of the physiology of the fallopian tubes that allowed the extraordinary advances in fallopian microsurgery.[7]

However, contemporary medicine must admit that in a number of cases sterility is incurable. In vitro fertilization appears to be an remedy in this situation, yet one must still recognize, moral considerations aside, that the success of this procedure is uncertain. Once the spectacular and almost magical appearance that this method offers to the public at large is dispelled, there remains the painful problem of sterility experienced by some couples. This is where we find a dimension of true suffering that some accept in silence, even solitude. Here also we find a factor that contributes to the passion of the debate. We must meet this problem with the deepest human compassion as well as concern for the broadest possible justice.

Accordingly, we regret the careless remarks often made by biotechnicians who reproach doctors opposed to IVF for being simplistic and lacking in understanding for human suffering. It would be just as great an error in judgment for a moralist to accuse, say, a cancer specialist of insensitivity to suffering because he rejects in vitro fertilization.

People are quick to forget that the procedure of in vitro fertilization poses truly grave ethical and moral problems to vast sectors of the medical corps because of its undeniable manipulation of embryos. Of course, the generosity, human warmth, deeply felt compassion and even charity made manifest by many of these doctors are concealed in this debate. This attitude is greatly deplorable.

3) Finally, we should realize that, in similar vein, procedures such as in vitro fertilization, the abortion of malformed infants, or euthanasia are not the only ones to offend the medical conscience in differing degrees. The World Association of Psychiatry, for example, raised its voice several times against the use of its specialty for the purposes of surveillance and repression. Other medical organizations have denounced doctors' participation in torture. On October 12, 1985, the Nobel Peace Prize crowned the efforts of thousands of doctors who, in the name of the most elementary good sense, gave the lie to the balance of nuclear power among nations. Really, how is it rationally possible to build peace among people on the entirely irrational concept of terror? In short, in vitro fertilization is far from monopolizing the preoccupation of doctors careful to protect human integrity from the delusions of a technology that is sometimes blown out of all proportion under the false pretenses of phony generosity, "security," or a vain search for peace.

D. There are in reality only *two problems* on which we must concentrate our questions:

1) Within what limits may a human being be *exposed* to technical procedures that present serious risk to his physical integrity and to his very existence?

2) Within what limits may a human being be *used*, with serious risk, to palliate a couple's sterility?

E. The irreducibility of the experimental manipulation that in vitro fertilization bears easily explains its condemnation by the "World Federation of Doctors Who Respect Human Life," at their congress in Ostend in October of 1984. This position, while rooted in biology, is also supported by the moral dimension Hippocrates gave to medicine, a dimension strengthened by the *Declaration of Geneva* (1948) and corroborated by article 3 of the *Universal Declaration of Human Rights* (UNO, 1948): "Every human being has the right to life." This position responds to the political trends laid bare by this new technology, trends that were pointed out by Dr. Schepens, General Secretary of the Federation, in a remarkable article.[8] We also discussed them the preceding chapter.

F. In order the better to understand our position, let us imagine the following situation: Mr. and Mrs. Dupont have adopted a Vietnamese child. What should they do, what would they do, morally speaking, if they knew beforehand, for example, that in crossing a raging war zone in very precarious conditions, the child would have but a 20% chance of arriving safely in their home?

3. THE BROKEN FAMILY

The problem of today's family must also be mentioned. A specialist made the alert observation that the technologizing of procreation leads couples gradually "to find themselves dispossessed of the creative relationship which they could build all throughout their personal history."[9] Nowadays it is possible to call a child into existence who would have three types of parents: genetic, gestational and socioeducational. J. F Malherbe's statement echoes those of Dr. Pierre Simon: "Sexuality will become disassociated from procreation and procreation from parenthood. The whole concept of family is in the process of collapsing. . . In a sense, all of society, through the mediation of medicine, will fertilize the couple."[10]

The former Grand Master of the Grand Lodge of France echoes a remark made by an obviously very important woman, but who did not give her name, at Royaumont, March 18, 1973, during the Colloquium of the Cercle de la Presse: "What we want to do is to destroy Judeo-Christian civilization. To do that we must destroy the family. To destroy the family we have to attack it at its weakest link. And its weakest link is the unborn child. Hence we are in favor of abortion."

All the more reason, then, for us to conclude that these sorcerer's apprentices will advocate the perfecting and dissemination of the new technologies precisely in order to precipitate the destruction of the family by striking at it through the weakest link they can find. Therefore, the moralist must guard against endorsing such doubly perverse medical practices: perverse because they make little of the human being at its most delicate stage of development, perverse because they lead to the abolition of the family.

In order to support this conclusion, we are going to show how in vitro fertilization attacks the two traditionally recognized ends of marriage: the founding of a family and the fulfillment of its members.

A. *Bringing Children into the World*

1. The couples that resort to in vitro fertilization seem to be — and undoubtedly think they are — giving an ethical welcome to a child in full accord with one of the essential ends of marriage. Upon reflection, however, it is clear that this is not so. The very fact that a couple is resorting to in vitro fertilization reveals a moral shift: instigated by medical practice, a principle of welcome has been exchanged for a principle of power. This change in ethical disposition also entails a change in disposition toward the embryo. The attitude of the spouses is no longer centered on the welcome of a *subject* who is awaited, instead it now concentrates on an *object* that satisfies a desire. The child is no longer considered a gift or even a grace, but as a right. Now, unless we wish to admit the legitimacy of slavery, a person may never be looked upon as an object or a right owned by someone else.

However, it could be said that the chance to procreate, to bring a child into the world who will be a testimony to love, belongs to every couple that experiences the desire. In this unfortunately very improper sense, we can speak of a "right to an infant." Yet we must wonder how far this "right" extends. We find two stances on this issue:

a) If one does not acknowledge an absolute right to procreation, then in vitro fertilization is morally unacceptable because it makes a human being deliberately run unjustifiable risks. Those who share this perspective, after invoking an absolute right to a child, should then find it unacceptable to introduce surreptitiously a right over the embryos deemed undesirable. For the human being thus tends to become an object to own, an object for which one pays ("the child at any price"), over which one has the advantage all the more easily in that the embryo is there, totally vulnerable in a glass dish , awaiting implantation, experimentation or destruction.

b) If one makes a child (a biological child, not an adopted child) an indispensable condition for the harmony of the couple, then for that reason in vitro fertilization is declared moral for a married couple.[11] If one adheres to the principle of efficacy at *any price*, one can envisage insemination by a third party,[12] uteri rented to raise the embryos, and, we never know, perhaps female animals as carriers of human embryos. . . In J. F. Malherbe's words, paradoxically, "the price of 'a child at any price' could result in the abolition of the family."[13]

In this second position, the absolute "right" of the couple to a child is guaranteed. This "right" calls for an embryo by means of in vitro insemination, embryo A, and necessarily prevails over the right to life of embryos B, C, D, etc., obtained in the same fashion and at the same time.

The rationale invoked for the sacrifice or abandonment of the extra, unused embryos could also be invoked for other cases. If we sacrifice embryos B, C, D, for A (for example, for need of "vital space"), or if we make them run unjustifiable risks, why, then, in that case, not sacrifice all of them for the sake of the mother? In other words, we can evidently sacrifice them in order to have none at all. The couple's will, desire, "right" is what rules. It is so easy to argue that it is the couple's right to want or not to want the child, and, consequently, to regulate by any means whatsoever the arrival of their offspring.

c) It follows that the principles that justify the elimination of useless embryos can be directly expanded to cover all human beings, regardless of their stage of development. That means that once the possibility, the probability (if not certainty) of their elimination is allowed as legitimate, then not only does abortion become admissible[14], but also the broad spectrum of techniques for euthanasia.[15] The green light has been given in particular to the early abortion pill (RU 486), whose praises are sung for us in its marketing.

2. The fact that they consider a child a right, an absolute right, or more exactly, that they consider the right to procreate an absolute right, leads to the sacrifice of an enormous number of existing human beings. This *paradoxical consequence* is confirmed by examining the actual procedure of in vitro fertilization.

a) The goal is to obtain a child, and so one must give it the most favorable odds possible. Hence one must, from the very beginning, envision several attempts at implantation before success can be assured. On the other hand, procuring eggs, while benefitting from simplified techniques, cannot be repeated without risk or damage. Furthermore, it is difficult, if not impossible, to preserve a non-fertilized egg at present. But one can very easily freeze and store embryos indefinitely.

The logic of efficacy demands that one obtain, fertilize, and freeze several eggs at the same time, in order to implant them successively until the pregnancy does succeed. The fate of the unfortunate "extra" embryos is left to the discretion of the doctors.

b) The goal is to obtain one and *only* one child. It is easy to see that the greater number of embryos implanted at the same time, the more chance of a successful operation. There is a 10 to 20% chance of success with the implantation of one embryo; 30% with two; 40% with 3, and so on. However, that does not mean that the chances of survival are improved for each of the implanted embryos, that each of them would have respectively a 30% or 40% chance of reaching term instead of the 10% it would have if implanted alone. No! There is always 10, 20, 30, or 40% chance that only one of the lot survives. However, while at times tolerated, multiple pregnancies are never sought for themselves and are sometimes terminated through "selective abortions."

c) Since the goal is to produce a *normal* child, a serious problem presents itself if one finds, or thinks he has found, an abnormal embryo.

Two cases must be considered:

—*Either* the parents will decide not to reimplant it, which is the most probable case since from the moment a couple accepts the principle of efficacy in calling a child into existence — with all the implications we have pointed out regarding the absolute "right to the child" — they reject any consideration of the fact that respect for the embryo's life is a primary moral imperative. The couple will, then, naturally tend to demand the same efficacy on the level of *quality* of the "product." What they want is a child at any price — so *long* as it is *normal*! If necessary, they will insist on having an examination of the amniotic fluid at the proper time.

—*Or* the parents will decide, rather extraordinarily, to have the embryo reimplanted. In such a case, they risk coming into conflict with the doctors who very probably will refuse to perform the operation. They will refuse for two reasons:

1) Due to their ethic of efficacy, the doctors will not authorize the existence of just any embryo, fetus or infant. They will make it a

question of honor to give birth to an infant beyond criticism. The intervention of the doctors is a whole: it is a question not only of calling a being into existence, but also one of quality.

2) In case of failure, they will be afraid of being sued (as is already the case in failed abortions) for not having produced the desired result. For along with the "evolution" of medical practice, one must attend to the "evolution" of jurisprudence.

d) In conclusion, if the embryo or fetus obtained by means of in vitro fertilization is malformed or there are strong indications that it will be, then they will almost unquestionably resort to *"retrieving"* it by means of an abortion.

In vitro fertilization, in its procedure as well as in the mentality that it presupposes and produces, leads the couple to no longer respect the life of the great number of embryos it conceives — in direct contradiction to its procreative end.

e) Let us again add that the argument generally invoked to "justify" this loss of human lives will not stand up to examination. According to some people, in vitro fertilization in effect does no more than *imitate nature,* which everybody knows does not hesitate to sacrifice a large number of fertilized eggs: according to the data recently published by Lancet, Dr. Schepene cites 8%,[16] as for Ch. Levevre,[17] the percentage goes up as far as 56%.

Such an argument is based on a regrettable confusion. In our philosophical tradition, different tendencies aside, whenever we confront human action there is a question of morality: every human act has a moral dimension. Consequently, if nature acts, no moral sense is involved; if man acts by means of his technology, he is morally implicated. That is the whole difference between *in vivo* and *in vitro*.[18] That is why in vitro fertilization cannot, without further ado, be considered as the direct extension and perfecting of artificial insemination techniques.

Here the immorality is twofold:

1) It is immoral *to call human beings into existence* knowing what inadmissible risks they will run. Right there — among others — we see a direct consequence of the Catholic Church's teaching on the motivations that make responsible parenthood a moral obligation.

2) It is immoral to increase *nature's violence* by organizing artificially, as it were, the conditions of an intrauterine selection as blind as it is pitiless.

B. *Fulfillment of the Spouses*

Having shown how in vitro fertilization leads to insurmountable contradictions from the point of view of one of the essential ends of marriage, that is, bringing children into the world, we will expose how it also can be an obstacle to the other essential end of marriage: the happiness of the spouses and all the members of the family.

1. From this point of view, there arises the problem of interference by a third person in the most intimate, the most interpersonal and the most creative relationship of the couple. Now the intervention of this third person is not accidental, but determinant. The doctor (or the medical team) intervenes on two decisive levels: it is the doctor who calls forth the new human being(s) into existence; it is the doctor who has the power to exercise control over the quality of the beings thus produced.

In such an intervention the parents, that is, those who furnish the gametes, are given no chance to participate or exercise control although, by definition, this possibility is inscribed in the conjugal relationship.

On the contrary, the doctor has a clear awareness of the "paternal" implication of his intervention, although he does not furnish the germinal cells. He is presented as the "father" of such a "test-tube baby." The parents produce the gametes, but it is the doctor who joins them. How can we speak of the child as issuing from an act of love? To take away from the couple the most creative dimension of their life in common is all the more offensive because it is done for the profit of someone who assumes none of the responsibilities or duties — those implied in becoming a parent — towards the embryo.

2. The presence or the memory of this alien intrusion into the very heart of the spousal and parental relationship runs the risk of entailing serious disturbances in the subsequent relationship of the couple.

a) Within the couple, negative psychological consequences are all the more probable in that a decision of this kind is rarely made equally. If one party wants the in vitro fertilization and the other party is only content to accept it, reproach is sure to follow.

b) The relationship between the couple and the child will be all the more difficult insofar as the couple will tend to look upon the child as their "thing," called into life in response to their desire. Furthermore, if the child does not match their hopes, the odds are great that they will begin to wonder about the child's origin. The suspicion will arise: "Can we trust this doctor, this medical team? Did they not make a deal?"

c) The *child* will also develop suspicions. He or she will have doubts about his or her origins and will raise the question of identity. The child has the right to be born in a normal way. It is profoundly unjust to impose upon him or her an invincible uncertainty as to origin and identity. Soon the family will be divided — the surest obstacle to the fulfillment of its members.

d) If, in conformity with what some people wish to happen, *the current tendency to disassociate "genetic" parentage, "gestational" parentage and "socioeducational" parentage intensifies, the family will suffer the consequences and will necessarily end in disintegration.* Some of those who hold to the new morality and some prophets of the new society, do not hesitate, as we saw above, to acknowledge that this is precisely the objective of the operation.

But then, deprived of all natural solidarity, the person will find himself reduced to abject *poverty* the more so in that poverty means vulnerability. Marx' proletariat still had their children as their only riches. . . Whence comes the anti-Malthusianism of the author of the *Communist Party Manifesto*. On the other hand, the contemporary problem forces the individual into the most precarious situation , since it deprives him of all control over *his own concrete future*, over a real future for his offspring: a kind of *alienation* heretofore unknown.

Added to the future alienation is the present alienation for woman. From the rank of mother she effectively becomes a mere donor of an egg, a renter of a uterus (with all the physical and moral suffering this implies), an object of every kind of pleasure. In short, the woman is no longer regarded as a person. The "master" makes her an instrument, and once again, she assimilates this viewpoint, regarding herself as truly being of the same value as the "master" has allotted her.

As far as children born of test-tube experimentation by the will of the masses are concerned, forever ignorant of the identity of her biological parents or of his gestational parents, both are well readied for the total surrender proper to all slaves.

4. RISKS AND POLITICAL RESPONSIBILITIES

The political dimension of this debate has been amply explained in the preceding chapters. In order to make our inventory of data regarding the problem as complete as possible, let us look once more at four points in this respect.

A. First, one would have to be either unconscious or irresponsible not to recognize the grave risks of *eugenics* that underlie the perfection and dissemination of the technique of in vitro fertilization. In a series of conferences devoted to these questions by Belgian Television at the time of the news on January 18, 1985, at 8:30 p.m., Dr. Brat, a gynecologist, did not hesitate to evoke the specter of Adolph Hitler. Without realizing it (for there are other fish to fry), Hitler is the one whom some doctors — and not just a few — are trying to re-animate in their mastery, with the blessing of thoughtless accomplices or moralists. Thanks to the sweet indifference of these doctors the door is wide open for a takeover, by the State or a dominant group, of human reproduction and the life of individuals. If we give free rein to their promoters, these biotechnologies will simply feed the dream of producing standardized individuals, identical, equal in the sense that they would be interchangeable: they would be *things*, no longer *personal* and different *Egos*.

B. The refusal to recognize certain categories of human beings provokes insurmountable contradictions on the legal level. These contradictions have already appeared in every country where abortion has been liberalized and protected by positive law. Now, this same refusal of recognition is a direct attack on the very essence of Western democracy. We are returning to the Athenian conception of democracy, according to which there are different categories of human beings. Plato, for instance, envisioned, due to arrested destiny, men with souls of gold, silver or bronze. At present, they argue from the real differences among men in order to provide a basis for legal inequalities and to translate these into practice.

But argumentation thus developed rests upon confusion between *equality* and *identity*. To say that men are equal does not mean that they are identical. When we speak of equality among men we mean that all have the same value, the same dignity by reason of being persons. But the very idea of person implies the idea of singularity, or difference. If we say that men are equal, we mean precisely that, regardless of the physical or intellectual difference observed among them, they all basically have the same value: They are equal *in dignity*.

The biotechnological procedures we examine are reintroducing the very principles upon which the Nazi regime was based. But those who ignore history are condemned to repeat its errors. They argue from real differences — and when necessary, assumed differences — among men in order to conclude from that statement, in itself rather banal, that an inequality of rights should correspond to those physical, intellectual, racial, etc., differences. By using such premises in their reasoning, they reintroduce into political society and into juridical institutions a pseudoaristocratic principle that the prophets and martyrs never ceased to denounce for its immorality, and against which western movements of resistance and revolution have always been organized.

And so, the partisans of these biotechnological procedures lose all credibility when they pretend to do justice to the rightful aspirations of the weakest.

C. This last remark finds another confirmation. The moralist must wonder about the importance given to a very expensive procedure in a society confronted with so many problems of *poverty* about which contemporary prophets constantly warn us.[19]

This raises the question of the origin of the financing of these feats, particularly within the context of containing university costs. Who finances them? The couples who benefit from them? Insurance companies? The State? Generous and misled patrons? What political options and intentions are at play here?

Society "mediated by the doctor" will be drawn more and more toward a fatal end: it will dispossess couples of their right to procreate. Since society will be called upon to pay for these procedures, it will decide the criteria of selection, of survival and of death.

In any case, since all scientific and medical research must be subject to moral judgment, this judgment must involve a veritable sorting-board of sociopolitical morality. We must examine the way to harmonize the rights of individuals with their obligations not only toward their regional or national community, but toward the fundamental human community.

D. We must add the fact that some biopolitical strategies propose directly to maintain Western hegemony over the Third World by *containing* their population as well as a racial *selection* whose name they don't dare mention. In this way economic aid often appears conditional on the use of a plan for limiting birth, regardless of the means (sterilizations en masse, voluntary or not, sanctions for the birth of a second or third child, etc.). The dissemination of "contragestives" (pills for *early* abortions: RU 486) will allow for the refinement of procedures already in progress, for these products can be administered to women without their knowledge. Some intrepid souls already even dream of bringing to the women of the Third World the embryos that Western women — at long last "liberated" — should not bear. . .

5. A NEW SCIENTISM?

A. In the discussion on in vitro fertilization we keep hearing that "science is not in a position to *decide* the question on the beginning of the human being, and would be incapable of saying *when* and *if* there is a human person present." This affirmation is both true and false.

— It is *true* to the degree that it falls outside the scientific domain to determine the nature, quality, and specificity of the human person, just as it is to affirm or deny the existence of God and the immortality of the soul.

— It is *false* because while strictly respecting method, science can say something about the *human individual*, mark its emergence, and analyze the genetic identity card or map that it will retain throughout its life. When sperm meets ovum, biologists can declare that an original new being begins at that moment, a being that has the genes not of a horse, not of a rabbit, but of a man, a being who will pursue his development for seventy or eighty years without interruption.

It would thus be sophistry to conclude that since science can say nothing about the human *person* as such, science cannot say anything about the human *individual*. As for affirming that the human individual necessarily has the ontological status of a person, this is a philosophical conclusion.

It would be a double sophism to conclude that since *science* cannot *say* anything about the human person as such, nobody, whether the man in the street, the philosopher or the theologian, can say anything about it. That would lead us back to a beautiful example of scientistic sophistry.

It would be a triple sophism to draw the *practical* conclusion that since science cannot *say* anything about the human person as such, the scientist can allow the threshold at which the human being must be respected to drift at his convenience — or that of his patrons or clients.

In any case, even assuming that the scientist must refrain from taking a theoretical position, he must still prudently conclude on the practical level that he must conduct himself as though he were dealing, without any doubt, with a human being. In the case of landslides, rescuers act on the hypothesis that there may be survivors, and they cannot be reproached for relentlessly continuing the search.

B. Once science assumes that it cannot decide the question of a human being's beginning and refuge is sought in the suspension of judgment, *practice becomes normative*. Ethics is no longer anything but the *reflection* of an entirely materialistic practice. What is done is good *because* it is done. Whence we have an irresistible spiraling: first abortion, then orthogenesis, in vitro fertilization, a call for third party donors, for gestational mothers, eugenics, euthanasia, etc. The *utility* of some becomes the criteria of *truth* for all.

They sometimes say that this is the price we must pay for scientific progress. They add that to take a position would be to " infringe upon academic freedom," and to "block the development of science." We have already seen that this type of argument does not survive examination. We might add here that the same logic is invoked for "justifying" war, "thanks to which incalculable scientific and technological progress is made."

These destructive statements demand the following responses:

1. The most costly *war* today in terms of human lives is not the (thus far) hypothetical one that would deploy nuclear weapons, among other sophisticated ones. No, the most deadly war is the one whose victims are found in laboratories and clinics, among millions of human embryos and fetuses.

2. This banalization of the deliberate killing of human beings gravely blunts the sensitivity of humanity's personal and collective moral conscience. It cripples the mechanisms of human reason that are capable, as Konrad Lorenz has shown,[20] of checking the aggressiveness which is part of man. Aggressiveness thus becomes unbridled, and we can foresee that it will lead to an increase of the kind of behavior that engenders wars. Mother Teresa has often made this point.

3. The manipulation of human embryos inescapably accustoms people to complacency in the face of murder of whatever kind. If I can dispose of the existence of a human being just conceived, one whom I can scarcely imagine but to whose presence science attests, why should I refrain from disposing of the existence of *any other* human being? Why should I not obliterate regions judged to be overpopulated, when that technique would be less burdensome than massive abortion and sterilization campaigns?

4. Milgram's famous experiments are very illuminating in this matter.[21] They invite us to remember that doctors, who share the human condition, can be led to *subject themselves to authority*. They remind us that man's aggressiveness towards his fellow creature is all the less restrained when this fellow human being is not perceived di-

rectly and/or is touched only indirectly. This is precisely the case here.

C. The debate on in vitro fertilization looks like a rehashing of old discussions about scientism. Yes or no, are the experimental methods of physics, chemistry, and biology the only valid methods of knowledge to which the human mind has recourse? Yes or no, should the last word on the dignity and destiny of man come from these disciplines?

Man will always remain a mystery to himself, a cipher that he must study. This mystery has to be discerned and probed by the intellect, employing for this purpose *convergent and complementary methods*. However, we must denounce the statement inherited from the tradition of scientism: "regarding the beginning of the human person, somewhat as in the case of God, science is not allowed to decide, and *as a consequence*, we cannot involve any scientific consideration that would provide the basis for a morality superior to experimental practice."

In short, biology can explain what an organism is and philosophy will tell us what a person is. But then why should it fall only to biologists to decide *in fact* that such and such a human individual has no right to respect?

D. Finally, it is necessary to avoid the pitfall of reenthroning an impossible dualism that smacks strongly of Manichaeism. We must dispute the pessimist vision that considers matter — particularly the body — as contemptible, and that, *therefore*, it can be manipulated amorally. In fact, under the guise of acting only on the body, the new technocrats touch the soul. Thus, if man is substantial unity, then we can never forget that what defines man is precisely that man rises above the matter that the biocrats depend on so heavily for their empire.

6. VETERINARIAN OR DOCTOR?

A. Like that concerning abortion, the controversy over in vitro fertilization requires that doctors rethink the specificity of their mission and weigh consequences of this mission on the plane of moral obligation. Medicine will make a false turn if, intoxicated by the upward spiral of performance, it endorses the scientistic premises of a certain kind of biology. Instead of treating patients with their own interests first and in harmony with medical moral obligation, it will drift towards a veterinary kind of morality.[22] One who cares for animals does so not out of the animal's interests, but those of the owner.

Doctor P. Simon, whom we already mentioned, takes this shift to its ultimate conclusion by introducing the concept of "medicine for the social body." [23] With perfect logic, the former Grand Master of the Grand Lodge of France places research for the good of the species above research for the good of the individual — morality of society above that of the person.

B. Medicine follows an equally false path if it introduces discrimination by reserving therapy only for certain categories of human beings, knowingly condemning others to experimentation or death. Medicine takes a false step if, forgetting the common good, it reserves the fruit of its achievements to a privileged minority of privileged nations, or if it promotes research programs in this direction. At that very moment it accepts, in fact, the role assigned to it in Plato's State.[24]

C. Today's advanced techniques allow doctors to *trespass* bounds they had been forced to surrender to — until now. This possibility places problems before doctors that they cannot resolve alone. We have a right to expect from them a sense of responsibility sufficient to recognize their lack of competence and to accept the principle of self-regulation and of interdisciplinary perspective. That is the *conditio sine qua non* of healthy discernment in foreseeable and morally acceptable hypotheses, experiments, or achievements, based on the respect due to every person from the first moment of existence.

D. If the powers of discernment are not employed, if doctors persist in resolving dilemmas case by case according to their passing inspiration, they will inevitably be caught up in the effects of a serpentine path which, having led them from abortion on demand to "liberating" euthanasia, will lead them from in vitro fertilization to the State's takeover of reproduction, via systematic eugenics. Doctors and Christian hospitals, in particular, must refuse to become involved lest they lose their specific character in short order.

7. THE CATHOLIC MAGISTERIUM: LANDMARK POINTS

A. It is proper to bring a theological clarification in this debate to the attention of Christians and non-Christians alike. While recalling that the child is "the most excellent gift of marriage,"[25] it is also appropriate to admit that, until now, the pope has rarely spoken on the problem of in vitro fertilization.

Some people believe they can use an interview published on August 1, 1978, by Cardinal A. Luciani as an argument in favor of their stance. Because of its importance and because of the way the text has been manipulated, a complete translation can be found at the end of this chapter.[26]

By generally limiting themselves to quoting the second paragraph of this interview, they remove it from a context that clarifies it. However, it is outright distortion to employ this text as an approval of in vitro fertilization. The future John Paul I begins the interview by describing the conditions in which he is expressing himself: in fits and starts over the telephone in a hospital room. He then makes clear in what capacity he is expressing himself: not as a bishop, but as a journalist consulted by his colleagues. In such a delicate and new matter, he too awaits the pronouncement of the authentic Magisterium of the Church.

With these preliminary warnings, he develops his response through four points. Cardinal Luciani first of all calls to mind the ambiguity of human progress: if in vitro fertilization does not provoke disasters, the least that can be said is that it encompasses great risks for the family and society. Secondly, the Patriarch of Venice sends his best wishes to the tiny English baby just born. As for her "parents," he has no right to condemn them, for they had a right intention and acted in good faith. They could even have great merit before God for what they decided to have the doctor do. It is this second point that is often quoted.

In the third paragraph Cardinal Luciani considers the deed itself, leaving aside the question of good faith, and looks at the moral problem squarely in one of its essential aspects: is extra-uterine fertilization legitimate? Following the teaching of Pius XII, Luciani asks whether it is permissible to admit artifice when, instead of being an extension of the conjugal act, the procedure in question completely excludes it. Luciani replied that in this case, the artificial technique is illicit because God has bound the transmission of human life to conjugal sexuality. He finds no valid argument on this point for deviating from the norm enunciated by Pius XII.

Based on this moral reference, the Cardinal Patriarch completes the positions he mentioned in the first and second points of the interview. Morality is concerned with human actions, actions through which persons can make good or bad use of scientific accomplishments. Each man must follow his conscience, but his conscience must be properly formed. Conscience does not create the law; it must first be informed by what God's law says and verify whether a particular action is in accord with that law.

B. Therefore, two points must be recalled in this regard. The first is that the constant teaching of the Church, and most especially that of John Paul II, has been that the two ends of marriage — procreation and fulfillment of the spouses — are inseparable. In vitro fertilization aims precisely at effecting procreation outside the act of reciprocal physical giving that expresses and makes real the spouses' commitment of love in an incomparable way. Over and above the questions concerning this procedure of procreation (since bringing one embryo to term necessarily entails the sacrifice of several others), we must remember that in vitro fertilization presupposes the intervention of a third person in the founding relationship of the family cell. This intervention on the part of a third person — in this case, the medical team, to say nothing of the donor of semen or egg, the brooder, etc. — initiates the process of shattering the couple and the family, as described by P. Simon and J. F. Malherbe.[27]

Secondly, contrary to what some people are willing to admit, recent discoveries make the task of the moralist much easier than formerly, in a way. If scientists can come to note the presence of a human being from the very beginning, the least moralists must do is insist that those beings have the same dignity and rights as others. We can understand, then, the prudence of pontifical declarations which do not speak of in vitro fertilization, but of "experiments in vitro" and of "genetic manipulations." [28] Regarding the first, John Paul II, who knows the meaning of words, affirms: "to conclude these personal reflections, showing how much I approve and encourage your praiseworthy research, I reaffirm that all of it must be subordinated to moral principles and values that respect and realize the dignity of man in its fullness." [29]

In this matter where sexual morality and social morality are tightly interwoven , there is no possible Christian position that would call into question either the inseparability of the two ends of marriage, or the absolute respect due to persons from the moment they exist. The most ancient tradition as well as contemporary science both point in exactly the same direction.

C. Hence, it is difficult to see how the supreme Magisterium could approve practices on which directly concerned ecclesiastical authorities, in different ways, have expressed great reservations.[30] Let us limit ourselves to mentioning the Australian bishops of the Victoria Province (where the most advanced experiments have taken place),[31] Cardinal Basil Hume[32] and the bishops of Great Britain in their reply to the Warnock Report.[33] The "perverse effects" of this practice have also been pointed out by the French episcopate's Commission on the Family,[34] and sporadically by Bishop Vilnet, the president of the episcopal conference of France.[35] Note also the declaration of the assembly of German bishops directed toward the "protection of the unborn child."[36] Finally, one should refer to the pages devoted to these questions by Cardinal Ratzinger.[37]

It goes without saying that these stated positions only anticipate new declarations of the Magisterium.

Let us add that the discretion of certain local episcopates confronted with this problem appears all the more regrettable in that it could encourage the establishment of a "parallel Magisterium," similar to that already denounced by John Paul II at Puebla. This situation would be aggravated all the more if, after the papal declaration to be made on this subject, pastors turn a deaf ear to them by advising the faithful to follow their conscience while "being respectful of Roman authority." They would thus consecrate moral subjectivism, confirm the myth that there are no norms, weaken the authority of the supreme Magisterium and hence their own authority.

In this regard, it is appropriate to remember that the bishops assembled in Rome for the Synod on the family from September 26 to October 25, 1980, expressly approved the teaching of *Humanae Vitae.* This position statement appears explicitly in two places: in Proposition 21 and in the final Message at no. 9. John Paul II in no. of 29 his Apostolic Exhortation *Familiaris Consortio* (November 22, 1981), quotes Proposition no. 21 of the Synod Fathers. By that very fact the earlier episcopal declarations on this question are now taken up and reinterpreted as part of *Familiaris Consortio.*[38]

8. SUMMARY

A. In vitro fertilization, first of all on the *philosophical* plane, gives rise to serious problems of an ethical and political order. It calls into question the basic principle in all human ethical systems, the foundation of all civilized societies: the Golden Rule. "Do unto others as you would have them do to you," a rule that Kant, among thousands, interprets this way: "Always act in such a way as to treat the humanity within you and others as an end and not simply as a means."

B. In vitro fertilization opens the way to the destruction of the family via reproduction itself as well as by means of the *socialization* of reproduction.

C. The development of new (existent and anticipated) biotechnologies, soon and in a fantastic way, will amplify the political and legal difficulties already observed in our examination of the social, political and juridical risks due to the liberalization of abortion.

D. In vitro fertilization provides a gauge for the *discretionary powers* held by higher ranking technicians who are caught up in the whirlwind of efficacy, but who are sometimes imprisoned in amorality.

E. These technicians offer leaders or powerful minorities unheard of *instruments of domination*, which will proceed from complete control over human reproduction, through eugenics, to end in programmed dying.

F. Finally, from the point of view of moral theology, it is urgent to give swift justice to the tiresome canard that in vitro fertilization is an open question, one to be decided by each individual choosing his own truth in a beautiful "pluralist" display. All the necessary principles are at hand in order to solve this problem, and there is no place whatsoever for a "new ethic" or a "new morality."

9. CONCLUSION: NO TO ASCENDANT AMORALITY!

Our study of in vitro fertilization's different implications emphasizes the solidity of the *moral criteria* we must take into account in order to make well founded ethical judgments about biotechnological procedures. It should never be a question of regarding the right to freedom in scientific research as an absolute, nor, above all, of using it as the ultimate criterion for scientific morality.[39] Unfortunately, in following these problems even briefly, we soon get the feeling and then the conviction that the areas of biological research under consideration here are the *headquarters* of ascendant amorality. Only ability, performance, *progress* counts. "If we don't do that, others will beat us to it. If we don't try this, we risk letting others *get ahead* of us." The researcher's freedom is unlimited, whatever is possible or seems doable is permissible and even desirable without restriction or condition. The freedom granted to scientists is absolute, often with the endorsement of poorly informed pastors or of moralists who fail in their role. The scientist is consecrated as unaccountable. Pastors and moralists thus contribute greatly to imprisoning scientists in pure biology, pure politics, pure positive law.

To the degree that moralists exclude any normative intervention, they automatically contribute to the generalized moral positivism that floods the entire fields of biology, law and politics. However, moralists just might remind themselves of what they should be reminding others, namely, of the primacy of the human individual, regardless of his or her stage of development. It is in this very primordial recognition that all interpersonal relationships are rooted.

If moralists out of guilt over the Galileo affair choose to sidestep the issue, they become de facto accomplices in the unbridled and irresponsible folly that has already invaded laboratories, hospitals and innumerable dispensaries. Some pastors and moralists, already intimidated by the noisily reported facts, fall into an even greater stupor since they often adopt an inferiority complex before laboratory technicians. Nevertheless, they must refuse to worship the modern Golden Calf whose power rests on the dominance of new biotechnologies.[40] If not, they will open wide the way for other Hitlers and Stalins at the close of our century, whether through ignorance, compromise or failure in duty.

We see from this that the moralist's task expands to new and unsuspected breadth. The attitude toward human life has become the touchstone of all morality. It governs both private as well as social morality. The lessening of respect for the human individual points *ipso facto* to the disappearance of the meaning of personhood. When I impose myself as the measure of another individual's existence, the sense of morality is dissolved and with it, the sense of sin. When we act as creators and proprietors of the genetic patrimony that we solely transport, then the sense of finiteness, the sense of creation and the sense of Providence vanish.

When through his actions and thought man has extirpated from mind and heart all idea of loving, parental, fraternal and existential relationships, he finds himself naked and in the tragic condition of a solitary individual that is vulnerable and exposed to the power of his rivals — and at the same time as a lord without pity, to the degree that he can wield his power over others.

10. APPENDIX: THE INTERVIEW WITH CARDINAL LUCIANI

We present here the complete text in English of Cardinal Luciani's interview which appeared in *Prospettive nel mondo* on August 1, 1978, and was reprinted in Venice's *Rivista diocesana* of September-October 1978. The translation is from the text found in the work of D. Tettamanzi (see note 26 of this chapter).

It is not easy for me to reply to your question this way, in fits and starts over the telephone, from a hospital room in which I find myself, without books that I can consult. And that is not the only difficulty. I have not read even a newspaper account about the "little English test-tube girl." In order for me to make a pronouncement over and above newspapers reports , I would need to know the scientific data established by the two doctors concerned with the case. That is not all; at this moment I am not speaking as a bishop, but only as a journalist consulted by a colleague. In a matter so delicate and quasi new, I my self await what the authentic Magisterium of the Church will declare once the experts are consulted. So my response to your question is personal, to my own risk and peril, and, I would say, "provisional."

I would make the following four points:

1) I share only in part the enthusiasm of those who applaud the progress of science and technique resulting from the birth of the tiny English girl. Progress is a lofty and beautiful thing, but not all progress is of profit to man. Atomic, bacteriological and chemical weapons were progress, but at the same time were a disaster for mankind. The possibility of having children in vitro — if that in itself does not provoke disaster — in any case poses immense risks. For example, natural fertility sometimes produces malformed children; does artificial fertility not risk producing even more? If so will not science, now face-to-face with new problems, seem like the sorcerer's apprentice who unleashes powerful forces without being able even to manage or control them? Another example: even considering the allure of profit and the absence of actual moral prejudice, is there not the danger of a new industry of "fabricating infants," perhaps for someone who cannot or will not contract a valid marriage? If that happened, would that not be a terrible setback instead of progress for the family and society?

2) In most cases, the press has congratulated the English couple and relayed best wishes to their infant. Following God's example, who wills and loves the life of men, I send my cordial wishes to the child as well. As for the "parents," I have no right to condemn them. Subjectively, they acted with right intention and in good faith and can have great merit before God for all they have decided and asked the doctors to do.

3) However, addressing the act itself and leaving aside good faith, the moral problem posed is whether extrauterine fertilization, in vitro or test tube, is proper. Speaking of artificial fertilization in marriage, Pius XII — if memory serves me well — made the following distinction. Does the intervention of the technician or doctor serve only to facilitate the conjugal act? Or does this intervention help to obtain a child by continuing in some way an already consummated marital act? There is no moral difficulty with that; the inter-

vention can be performed. On the other hand, far from helping or prolonging the conjugal act, does the artificial procedure exclude it entirely and replace it? Then it is not correct to allow the artificial, because God has bound the transmission of human life to conjugal sexuality. Thus spoke Pius XII, pretty nearly; and I find no valid arguments to allow me to set that norm aside by declaring it licit to separate the transmission of life from the conjugal act.

4) Furthermore — I read this in a newspaper — "it is ridiculous to speak of moral problems to someone who profits from magnificent scientific feats. And then there are the rights of free individual conscience." Very well, but morality is not concerned with the feats of science; it is concerned with human actions, with the way that people use scientific achievement for good or ill. As regards individual conscience, we agree: it must always be followed, whether it commands or forbids. The individual, nonetheless, must see to it that he has a well formed conscience. It is actually not the role of conscience to create law. It has two duties: first, to be informed of what God's law says; then, to judge whether a specific action on our part is in accord with that law. In other words, conscience must command man, not obey man.

Endnotes for Chapter III:

[1] This chapter draws conclusions principally from a series articles published by authors of different tendencies in the Belgian daily, *La Libre Belgique* (Brussels), between December 1984 and February 1985. We will make, therefore, references to this newspaper, citing it as *LLB*. This text was published before the Instruction *Donum Vitae* (Feb. 22, 1987).

[2] The expression is that of J. F. Malherbe, Director of the Centre d'Etudes de Bioéthique affiliated with the Catholic University of Louvain (cf. *LLB* Jan. 11, 1985). Regarding some positions taken by the members of the CEB, there is a publication available for public use. We are indebted to Edouard Boné and Jean-François Malherbe for *Engendrés par la science*, an amazing work having as its object the *Enjeux éthiques des manipulations de la procréation*. This volume appeared in the Collection Recherches morales. Positions (Paris: Cerf, 1985). On this work see P. Favraux and A. Chapelle, "Bioéthique et foi chrétienne. A propos d'un livre récent," *Nouvelle Revue théologique* 108 (March-April 1986) 249-267. One can complete this by referring to the unequal dossier, "Vers la 'procréatique'. Une société ou les enfants viennent par la science," a special issue of the review *Projet* #195 (Sept-Oct 1985). To the latter one can add the interviews gathered by Emmanuel Hirsch in *Des motifs d'espérer? La procréation artificielle*, Coll. Recherches morales (Paris: Cerf, 1986). One should note above all the contributions of Claude Bruaire, "Réflexions d'un philosophe," 71-82, and Catherine Labrusse-Riou, "Etre juriste et membre du comité national d'éthique," 131-159. Lastly, in J*AMA (Journal of the American Medical Association)* 11:123 (May 15, 1986), Terra Ziporyn writes that "'The artificial reproduction of man poses some medical and social problems" (525-530).

[3] The difficulties that some contemporary authors stumble upon regarding individuation and animation can be explained in part by their (often unconscious) attachment to the old Cartesian dualism. With such premises, how can we rediscover the doctrine of substantial unity? Ontology is one of the fundamental disciplines of philosophy. Without entering into too much detail, let us say that it "has as its object beings in themselves and

not as they appear or their phenomena." Cf. Paul Foulquié, with the collaboration of Raymond Saint-Jean, *Dictionnaire de la langue philosophique* (Paris: Presses Universitaires de France, 1962) 497. See also Ph. Caspar, "*Individuation des êtres*," cited in Ch II, note 7.

[4] This is the position of J.M. Hennaux and of Dr. Ph. Schepens. It also appears in R. Jordens (cf. *LLB* 4, 12, 13 and 23 of Jan. 1985.). Since then, J. M. Hennaux has developed his thought in two articles: "Fécondation in vitro et hôpitaux catholiques," in *Vie consacrée* 57 (1985) 77-110; and in "Fécondation in vitro et avortement. Simple note morale au sujet de la Fivete," in *Nouvelle Revue théologique* 108 (Jan-Feb. 1986) 27-46. See also Jérôme Lejeune and Geneviève Poullet, Maternité sans frontières (Paris: Ed. VAl, 1986); Bernard Martino, Le Bébé est une personne (Paris: Ed. Balland, 1986). See also Jérôme Lejeune "Biologie et personne humaine," an extract from *Revue de la Recherche juridique. Droit prospectif*, published by the Faculty of Law and Political Science of Aix-Marseille (Aix-Marseille: Presses Universitaires, 1985).

[5] Cf. Ch. Lefèvre in *LLB* of Jan. 10, 1985.

[6] Cf. *L'Homme manipulé*, ed. by Charles Robert, Recherches européennes, Strasbourg, Sept. 24-29, 1973. Coll. Hommes et église, 6, Université des sciences humaines de Strasbourg (Strasbourg: Cerdic, 1973). Prof. Férin's text can be found on pp. 25-34. Let us point out here that Pierre Thullier devoted an interesting dossier to "L'Expérimentation sur l'homme," in *La Recherche* 179 (Paris, July-Aug. 1986) 952-965; he also provides some bibliography.

[7] Among numerous examples of disinformation that she mentions in her thesis (cited in note 15), Patricia Soutoul recalls the systematic concealment of two of the greatest causes of sterility: sexually transmitted diseases and abortion, whence the importance of the prevention of sterility.

[8] Most of the Acts of the Congress can be found in *News Exchange of the WFDRHL*, a review published in both French and English (address: H. Serruyslaan, 76, B 8400 Oostende). See above all nos. 85 of Feb 1985, 86 of March 1985, and 87 of May 1985. The text of the *Déclaration* to which we refer is found in *News Exchange*, n. 85 of Feb. 1985, p. 8 (see also p.7); the same references exist for the English version of this review. Dr. Philippe Schepens points out the "trends" mentioned here in *LLB* of Jan 23, 1985.

[9] *LLB* of Jan. 11, 1985.

[10] P. Simon, *De la vie avant toute chose* (Paris: Mazarine, 1979). In some of the first kibbutzim, children's education was completely in the hands of the community. This experiment naturally entailed a radical calling into question of the traditional family. By changing the environment and in particular through education, they hoped to bring about a "new man." This experiment should be clarified with the help of the celebrated study of David Riesman, La foule solitaire. *Autonomie de la société moderne*, Coll. Notre Temps, 9 (Paris: Arthaud 1964); see especially the pages devoted to "external determination," *passim*. One of the reference works on the experiment of community education in the kibbutzim was produced by Bruno Bettelheim, *Les enfants du rêve*, Coll. Reponses (Paris: Robert Laffont, 1983); he also offers an important bibliography. The role of the family in the education of the child has often been studied. See, for example: Claude Lévi-Strauss, *Les structures élémentaires de la parenté* (Paris: Presses Universitaires de France, 1949); Paul A. Osterrieth, *L'enfant et la famille*, Centre d'entraînement aux méthodes d'éducation active, New edition (Paris: Scarabée, 1967); Idem, *Faire des adultes*, Coll. Psychologie et sciences humaines, 7, 7th edition (Brussels: Dessart, 1969); Berthe Reymond-Rivier, *Le développement social de l'enfant et de l'adolescent*, Coll. Psychologie et sciences humaines, 11 (Brussels: Dessart, 1965); René A. Spitz, *La première année de la vie de l'enfant: genèse des premières relations objectales*, Coll. L'actualité psychanalytique (Paris: Presses Universitaires de France, 1958); Id., *De la naissance à la parole. La première année de la vie* (Paris: Presses Universitaires de France, 1968); Henri Wallon, *L'évolution psychologique de l'enfant*, Coll. U Prisme, Education-Psychologie, 3 (Paris: Colin, 1981). We should also point out here that Gérard-François Dumont has made a lucid and realistic defense of the family in *Pour la liberté familiale* (Paris: Presses Universitaires de France, 1986).

[11] This is the opinion notably of R. Jordens (see *LLB*, Jan. 23, 1985) and J. and P. A. Veldekens (see *LLB*, Jan. 23, 1985).

[12] As does Dr. Brosens (see *LLB*, Jan. 11, 1985).

[13] See note 2, *supra*.

[14] See the warnings of J. M. Hennaux in *LLB*, Jan. 23, 1985); cf. also the articles by the same author cited in note 4.

[15] Cf. the proposed law for Belgium presented in Parliament by M. D'Hose on Jan. 21, 1985.

[16] Article was cited in note 8.

[17] *LLB* Jan. 19, 1985.

[18] See in this Chapter, 10. Appendix.

[19] See the article by Dr. Schepens cited in note 8.

[20] Cf. Chapter XIII, entitled, "Ecce Homo" in *L'agression. Une histoire naturelle du mal*, Nouvelle Bibliothèque Scientifique (Paris: Flammarion, 1969) 251-289.

[21] Cf. Stanley Milgram, *Soumission à l'autorité. Un point de vue expérimental*, 2nd edit. (Paris: Calmann-Levy, 1984).

[22] Some clear-sighted veterinarians were among the first to perceive the dangers of transposing their accomplishments among animals to the human species Their warning is especially relevant to embryology. See, for example, the article of Prof. Luc Henriet, "Réflexions après un Congrès historique," in *La Libre Belgique* of Jan. 22, 1981.

[23] *Op. cit* 53. Cf. Ch. Lefèvre, *LLB* Jan. 13, 1985.

[24] Cf. e.g., *The Republic* III, 406e; 409 e - 410 a.

[25] *Gaudium et spes*, 50.

[26] The text of Cardinal Luciani's interview appears first in *Prospettive nel mondo* of August 1, 1978, and was reprinted in *Rivista diocesana* of Venice, Sept-Oct. 1978. It can also be found in the valuable work of Dionigi Tettamanzi, *Bambini fabbricati: Fertilizzazione in vitro. Embryo Transfer.* Coll. Azione pastorale (ed. Piemme di Pietro Marietti, 1985). See 170-172. The value of this work is twofold: it contains, first of all, the positions explained by Prof. Tettamanzi himself; it also contains the collection — made by the celebrated Italian moralist in a long appendix (pp. 157-210) — of the texts of the Church's Magisterium that are very important in our discussion of this subject.

[27] See *supra*, 64 ff.

[28] Regarding this, see 'L'Allocution à l'association médicale mondiale," in *Documentation catholique* 1863 (Dec. 4, 1983) 1068.

[29] "L'expérimentation en biologie doit contribuer au bien intégral de l'homme," discourse of Oct. 23, 1982 before the Pontifical Academy of Science, in *Documentation catholique* 1840 (Nov. 21, 1982) 1028 f.

[30] Regarding the positions of those mentioned, special importance attaches to that of Msgr. Carlo Caffara in *L'Osservatore Romano* of Nov. 29, 1978. An authority if there is one in this field, Msgr. Caffara also gave a remarkable conference in Paris, on Nov. 16, 1985, at the Sixth National Colloquium of Catholic Lawyers; it was devoted to biology, morality and law on prenatal life. It bears the title "La procréation artificielle face à la théologige morale," and is available from the Confédération des juristes catholiques de France, 3 ave. Robert Schuman, F 13628 Aix-en-Provence.

[31] Cf. *Documentation catholique* 1883 (Nov. 4, 1984) 1021- 1024.

[32] *Ibid.* 1020 f.

[33] Cf. *ibid.* 1893 (April 7, 1985) 3920401.

[34] Cf. *ibid.* 1885 (DEc. 2, 1984) 1126-1130.

[35] Cf. *ibid.* 1904 (Oct.20, 1985) 981.

[36] Cf. *ibid.* 1908 (Dec. 15, 1985) 1162-1164.

[37] Cf. Joseph Ratzinger and Vittorio Messori, *Entretien sur la foi* (Paris: Fayard, 1985) esp. 95-114.

[38] Cf. "Les 43 propositions du synode des evêques sur la famille," in *Documentation catholique* 1809 (June 7, 1981) 537-550; The 21st Proposition is on page 543. See also "Message aux familles chrétiennes dans le monde d'aujourd'hui," ibid. 1796 (Nov. 23, 1980) 1047-1050; No. 9 is found on page 1048. l'Exhortation Apostolique Familiaris Consortio is found ibid. 1821 (Jan. 3, 1982) 1-37. In particular No. 29 says: "For this reason the Synod Fathers made the following declaration at their last assembly: 'This Sacred Synod, gathered together with the Successor of Peter in the unity of faith, firmly holds what has been set forth in the Second Vatican Council (cf. *Gaudium et Spes*, 50) and later in the Encyclical *Humanae Vitae*, particularly that love between husband and wife must be fully human, exclusive and open to new life' "(11, cf. 9, 12). *Familiaris Consortio* is available in English from the Daughters of St. Paul, 50 St. Paul's Avenue, Boston MA 02130. We must add to these documents the Congregation for the Doctrine of the Faith's *Declaration on Sexual Ethics*, Dec. 29, 1975, available from the United States Catholic Conference, 1312 Massachusetts Ave. NW, Washington DC 20005.

[39] Concerning the relationship between science and morality, John Paul II frequently offers explanations that apply to bioethics. For example, see "Einstein, Galileo," Discourse to the Pontifical Academy of Science in *Documentation catholique* 1775 (Dec. 2, 1979) 1009-1011; "La rencontre de la Science et de la Théologie," Discourse to a group of Nobel Prize Winners, *ibid.* 1800 (Jan. 18, 1981) 63-65; "Le service de l'homme à travers la science et la recherche," Homily at the Mass for university students, *ibid.* 1825 (March 7, 1982) 245-247; "Réflexion éthique et fidélité au Magistère et à la Tradition," Discourse to an International Congress of Moral Theology, *ibid.* 1918 (May 18, 1986) 483-485.

[40] John Paul II has often turned his attention to the new problems in medical ethics. See, e.g., "Liberté de conscience et défense de la vie," Allocution to Italian Catholic Doctors, *Documentation catholique* 1756 (Jan. 21, 1979) 51-53; "Discourse to doctors and surgeons," *ibid.* 1796 (Nov. 23, 1980) 1037-1039; "L'inviolabilité de la vie humaine," Discourse to the participants in the first Congress for the African and European Family, *ibid.* 1802 (Feb. 15, 1981) 158-159; "Le médecin au service de la vie," Discourse to the World Congress of Catholic Doctors, *ibid.* 1840 (Nov. 21, 1982) 1020-1032; "L'expérimentation en biologie doit contribuer au bien intégral de l'homme,' Discourse to the Pontifical Academy of the Sciences, *ibid.* 1840 (Nov. 21, 1982) 1028-1029; "L'intervention chirurgicale sur l'être humain avant sa naissance," Allocution to the International Medical Congress of the *Movement for Life*, *ibid.* 1863 (Feb. 20, 1983) 189-191; "Le médecin et les droits de l'homme," Allocution to the World Medical Association, *ibid.* 1863 (Dec. 4, 1983) 1067-1069. Recall also that John Paul II wrote a Letter, "Salvifici doloris," for *Sens chrétien de la souffrance humaine*, *ibid.* 1869 (March 1984) 233- 250. Finally, let us not forget the "Lettre sur quelques questions concernant l'eschatologie," of May 17, 1979, published by the Congregation for the Doctrine of the Faith, *ibid.* 1769 (Aug. 5-19, 1979) 708-710.

chapter IV

WHAT NEW POLITICAL WORLD ORDER?

In the history of political thought many sought the source of law in might. In the fifth century B.C., the Sophists saw the advantage or utility of the powerful as a driving force for political life. For Callicles, justice is determined by the will of the strongest.[1] Protagoras condenses all Sophist thought into a formula that lends itself to a variety of interpretations: "Man is the measure of all things."[2] Pushed to its furthest political consequences, this last adage is very disturbing: is everything subjective? Do I not have any point of reference other than myself? Am I myself the measure of others? Is the power that I have at my disposal sufficient in justifying my imposition on others? Is maximum pleasure the norm for my actions, or is it the utility that I can derive from it? Am I the measure of what is beneficial or good or just or, in the end, even of what *is*? In particular, does the existence of the other impose on me to the point that I must recognize him as another being, distinct from me? Can I refuse to acknowledge him as equal to me in dignity? By what right?

Our Sophists would have responded to all these questions based on the interests of x or the utility of y, thus expressing the prevailing opinion today which reflects the established practice of the Sophist environment.[3]

However, people were not slow to raise their voices against such assertions: Antigone, for example, whom Sophocles made to proclaim a justice higher than that of kings; Socrates, for another, affirms that every man, even a slave like Meno, is personally capable of discovering truth,[4] truth for which he is responsible and to which he must conform his actions, ready to let himself be condemned by the judges' invocation of a law that may be incontestable, but that is deprived of all legitimacy.[5]

The Sophist tendency is preserved today by all the partisans of what we may call "pure" politics, that is to say, in the fashion of Machiavelli and others who see authority only in terms of its usefulness and effectiveness; authority: how to acquire it and, once acquired, how to use it? Thus the exercise of authority leads to the use of force: if I am stronger, I can force or even induce others to act they way I want them to act. Note that we first said "force" and then "induce;" we must recognize the difference in nuance, the increasing reach implied by the order of these two verbs.

1. NEITHER FORCE. . .

In 1215, when the English barons foresaw what would become *habeas corpus* in 1679, they rebelled against the abusive and arbitrary restraints imposed on individuals (as well as wealth). Every Western revolution came about in this spirit, that is, in reaction against the tyranny of princes who viewed their capricious arrests as having the force of law. The times had come to the point where "whatever the tyrant in power wrote, that was called law." [6]

The political, legal and moral history of the West sought to check these princes' exorbitant claims. Little by little and at the cost of a long struggle, there came to light the idea that *all* men are free and equal in dignity. This concept affirms that this inalienable dignity must be universally declared and recognized as well as promoted everywhere in the world. Man is not moved simply by theoretical principles in the discovery of this concept. After a long period of maturation, this idea was solemnly proclaimed in the *Universal Declaration of the Rights of Man* of 1948.

To proclaim that all human beings are equal in dignity precisely because they are human beings is to denounce the pretensions of those who would reserve human dignity for members of such and such a race, nation, party, or "elite." It is to denounce the category of *Unmensch* developed by Naziism in order to justify the massacre of Jews, Ukrainians and migrants. We do not make such a denunciation arbitrarily; it is not inspired by utility or the interest of a particular group, nor is it even the expression of the "opinion" of a numerical majority. It is based on a truth before which we bow, a truth we affirm and proclaim. It is this primordial truth that will inspire political regimes to come, one that governments will make a commitment to promote.[7]

Thus we see that the discovery, formulation and proclamation of this truth that is the foundation of the new political world order, guarantor of enduring peace, is not simply the end result of philosophers' reflections. It is also the fruit of experience. Man draws his teaching from his own defeats and suffering. Thus did the Universal Declaration of the Rights of Man in 1948 draw its lesson from the second World War: it sorts out the causes and seeks a way forever to prevent such disasters.

Western history is marked by one constant: the refusal by the rest of society of repression at the hands of this or that prince, people, class, or minority, just as we denounce all arbitrary and exclusive power. In the name of respect for man, for his inalienable right to life, liberty and equality, we reject any proposal of domination, bondage, or subjugation.

2. . . .NOR INDUCE

However, not only can I force others to act for my own ends, I can also induce them to do so. I can induce others, not only to act, but to judge as well. This kind of domination is at once more cunning, more pernicious and more fatal in its effects. It is not at all new, but it has grown in an unprecedented way because of two decisive factors. On the one hand, it has benefitted from the use of the most sophisticated techniques of propaganda and indoctrination. On the other hand, its effectiveness is assured by the media's guarantee of publicity.

3. THE ESSENCE OF TOTALITARIANISM

Contemporary totalitarianism goes much further than did ancient despotism, the absolutism of yore, or the classical dictatorships. De Tocqueville envisioned the possibility that democracy could drift toward totalitarianism: "Absolute monarchies brought dishonor upon despotism; let us take care that democratic republics do not rehabilitate it and, by making it oppressive for a few, hide its hateful aspect and degrading character from the eyes of the many."[8]

For contemporary totalitarianism the question is no longer one of exercising physical coercion; henceforth it is a matter of destroying the Ego in what is most profoundly personal in me.[9] This is why contemporary totalitarianism has intellectual life as its target. It pummels the masses, but the intellectuals it reeducates by filtering, directing and dealing in information. It inculcates a portable ideology, for ideology can encroach upon intelligence and disarm its critical ability, imprisoning it in a "gulag of the spirit." Bit by bit, intellectuals are ensnared by manipulators of knowledge who are in the pay of the party, the race, the army, the powerful. Science is fostered to the degree that it delivers new technologies that can be integrated into a global strategy for domination.

This debilitation is no less dramatic on the moral level. Man has been dispossessed of all responsibility; he escapes the positive or negative consequences of his conduct and of whatever decisions are left to him. He is infantilized, and the planners, the technocrats, make decisions for him.

Thus vigilance, already extinguished at the level of intelligence and will, ends in extinction at the level of conscience as well.

This generalized alienation has direct relevance in the area that concerns us. Man, under the guise of being liberated and excited by the possibility of maximizing individual pleasure, disregards the stakes and consequences of sexuality. This trend did not escape Simone Veil: "One sees a certain tendency toward the privatization of sexuality and reproduction; they are regarded more and more as the affair of the couple alone, all the while the consequences (that is, the child) are more and more socialized."[10] The responsibility of the partners is transferred to technocrats and planners, thereby delivering a fatal blow that clears the way to the ruin of the institution of the family. We know that the destruction of the family to the benefit of the City and State was foreseen by the dictators of classical times as well as those imagined by Plato.[11]

But henceforth, it is no longer in the name of the City, State or race that individuals and couples are invited to make a gift of their germinal cells or to the sacrifice of themselves. The dominant theme must be the morality of the species. Up until now, the fashion was the "doctrine of national security" applied by military technocrats. [12] We are now witnesses to the emergence of a "doctrine of biological security" set up by medical technocrats.

4. FROM THE LIE. . .

The democratic ideal is founded, as we have seen, on the recognition of a primordial truth: the common dignity of each and every human being. Contrariwise, in order to justify the new morality, people resort to a classic totalitarian weapon: the lie. Since the 6th century B.C., Sun-Tzu regarded the lie as a means to subjugate the enemy without the force of arms.[13] For Plato, order in the City had to rest on a famous "noble lie."[14] Hitler built his whole delirious project on a few lies thinly disguised with jargon borrowed from biology, history and geography. Cynical nonsense that; he even remarked that the bigger the lie was, the more chance it had of being swallowed by the people. And although Stalin was as poor a geneticist as he was a linguist, we must recognize that he brought the combination of lies and violence to rare perfection.

5. . . .TO VIOLENCE

Now it is precisely this alliance between violence and lying that contemporary empires are in the process of redefining and reformulating.[15] Never has there been more frequent use of misrepresentation.[16] The most violent behavior is concealed with the language of liberation.

Lately abortion has been presented as "liberation" for women, and all the while it is one of the major conquests of male domination. Besides, the use of the term "liberation" is doubly derisive, since the cost of this pseudoliberation is the destruction of a human being. In vitro fertilization is presented as a remedy for sterility, while it consists in but distorting it and, in order to palliate its consequences, runs inadmissible risks of killing human beings in the earliest stage of their development. Experiments that necessarily entail the sacrifice of human beings are presented as indispensable to scientific progress and the welfare of man. They pretend that the liberalization of abortion has no effect on the birth rate. While affirming that these experiments are indispensable to science, they fail to say that they would be just as conclusive if they were carried out on animals. But of course human embryos cost less than monkey embryos. In order to save human beings, they take organs from other human beings that are sacrificed. Under the disguise of aid for development, international institutions, public and private, supported by governments, carry on campaigns of massive sterilization in the Third World. They present as a "right" for some what is only the expression of special interest for others. They present the "gift" of death as a liberation. "Freedom through death": now there is something here that revives strange memories. . .

In short, we are witnessing a triple perversion: that of language, that of intelligence, and that of the will. They call liberation what is actually servitude; they call life what is death; they call good what is bad. The lie runs to the help of violence, and violence flies to the aid of the lie.

6. DEMOCRACY ON TRIAL

There's nothing local about the problem that requires us to take a position. What is in question is the very essence of democracy. We simply have to guard and preserve this major conquest on the part of humanity: the sense of unconditional respect for every human being. We must not only defend against the ever renewed assaults on this conquest that is as practical as it is theoretical; we must also promote it on the political, legal, socioeconomic and cultural levels.

Democracy cannot flourish except where there exists a community of consciences that are both open to the truth *and* personally responsible. Just as democracy cannot be built on violence, it cannot be built on a lie either. The unshakable foundation of all true democracy is an elementary but decisive truth: all persons are equal in dignity. This proposition does not draw its force from the fact that it would be supported by a more or less comfortable margin in a vote. It demands respect and adherence by its intrinsic force. That is why it is "declared" and "proclaimed," and not "conceded" or "granted."

Thus democracy takes root in unanimity on a truth that is also its bedrock: the right of every human being to life and to the values that flow from it, namely, freedom and equality.

When, as is the case now, the consensus on this truth is seriously impaired, or this ultimate point of reference is infected with suspicion, when the definitions of man begin to multiply in geometric progression, then democracy is directly in danger.[17]

The weakness of democracy is that it rests on a truth concerning man, a truth to which men freely consent, but — and contemporary history confirms this — this truth has never been automatically assumed and concretized in positive law. In order to be inscribed in history and society, this law must, as has been widely the case up until now in our Western societies, be at the basis of all constitutions and of all positive law. To his honor, it is the specific task of the politician to see that the intimate connection between this truth and the law is never destroyed.

Even our Western democracies are slow to recognize the human being. He risks not being recognized as a human being unless he is granted the quality of citizen. Positive law can always confine or drive him back into the category of *Unmensch*. But if this is so, in what way are we to be distinguished from the Nazis? Why did we fight the war? In whose name have we denounced Auschwitz, and by what right do we condemn the gulag?

Moreover, when due to lies or suspicions law becomes separated from the truth-basis of democracy, then society teeters into anarchy. It no longer has a guiding principle that everyone accepts solely by virtue of the shining authority of its truth. It no longer has any other principle to command itself except the might of the strongest, whose insolent power is erected into a source of law. Everything can be made legal, even theft, terrorism and murder, when one rejects *in toto* the standard of what at least in democracies is the sole *raison d'être* of law: respect for every man.[18]

7. WHAT TOTAL WAR?

Some theoreticians of Naziism furnished Hitler and his imitators with the concept of "total war."[19] The war was indeed total in the sense that it unfolded on the political, economic, psychosocial, scientific and military plane. Between politics and war there wasn't just continuity, but one was reduced to the other, so to speak.

We are at the dawn of a total war beyond the limits of anything we have known, and the horizon is already aflame with it. The present war is truly total in the sense that, by means of power over life, it aims at control over hu man beings in what is most inalienable: their existence, their personal capacity for making judgments and decisions, and their responsibility before their conscience. The present war simultaneously involves each of these aspects as the stakes, the means and the goal.

8. WHAT TYPE OF SOCIETY TO PROMOTE?

The discussion on the particular problems of bioethics brings us right back, then, to an old, fundamental debate about man. What is my relationship to other men? Am I to be their measure?

The biomedical disciplines alone cannot give a final reply to these questions. The contributions of philosophers, political scientists, and especially of legal experts are indispensable. However, in one capital way, the progress of biomedical disciplines is of great assistance to the politician. In effect, it enables one to detect with precision the existence of a human being much sooner than we could in 1940. Contemporary genetics highlights the perfectly original and distinct character of the zygote, which will pursue its development without discontinuity until death.[20]

Hence, the sooner we discover this human being, the sooner we must recognize and respect him. There is no way that we can attack this principle or limit its implications without putting into motion a process that will degrade democracy to totalitarianism. It is then for even greater reason that we must vigorously and without fail insist that no technique, no matter how sophisticated, that no research, no matter how promising, justifies an experiment that endangers a human being, no matter how tiny. If in its essence democracy is the recognition of identical dignity in all men, its ruination is assured were we to exclude a particular category of human beings from this universal vision .

Thus there is really only one question facing the politician: what type of society do we want to promote? The politician's answer cannot entail following the herd which is so easy to fool. Nor can it consist in collaborating with those who, profiting from the complexity of biotechnological problems, deceive the public at large with the help of the media. On the contrary, politicians must anticipate the perils that menace society;[21] he must protect the fabric of society from the germ of corruption; he must screen the easily manipulated mass of citizens from the paralyzing conditioning of which they are the object.

Expressed in positive terms, the politician's tasks are summed up in only one: to safeguard the fundamental demand of justice, whose principle and end is the unconditional respect for every human being.

9. EUROPE BEFORE ITS DESTINY

In this regard, the European politician finds himself particularly challenged. By reason of the titles or roles that are properly his, he is the guardian of values that have been proven and promoted throughout history. The danger to which European politicians are exposed — a danger to which some seem already to have succumbed — is to be led to renounce their identity, their individuality. The risk is precisely that the institutions of European countries, as well as those of others, will become puppets under the surreptitious control of the high and mighty, yielding to the point of losing all initiative and being induced to agree to their own powerlessness.

Toward 1937 in Germany, all or almost all supported Hitler. But this mass rallying had been arranged by a long series of personal and institutional concessions — especially political ones.

Only a few "fools" who were particularly alert dared to understand and say no; many of these paid for their independence of spirit with their lives. For the rest, history abundantly testifies to the surrender of intellectuals and the blindness of politicians: here we see the litter spread by dictatorships and totalitarian regimes.[22]

So Europe is once again confronted with its destiny. But a new factor is emerging: Europe has begun to coalesce and even to redefine its destiny within the framework of community institutions. Everything impels it to embrace its historical responsibilities anew. We will examine these responsibilities of Europe first on the level of Europe itself, then from the viewpoint of the relationship between Europe and the Third World. In both cases, these responsibilities call for choices to be made.

10. A CHANGE THAT IS NOT FATAL

In one choice, Europe can consent to servitude and to see ing itself through borrowed glasses; it can assent to induced behavior and allow its economy, media, universities and institutions to be placed under a protectorate.[23] Socioimperialism and the rival yet somewhat conniving versions of worldwide messianism are both there, fascinating, each one with its objectives, methods, weapons — and commandos.

The question is simple: are we going to secure the posthumous victory of Naziism? Are we going to enthrone a political system and a morality for our species that limits itself to the management of human cattle? For that is exactly where our present laissez-faire attitude in biopolitics inexorably leads. We must have the courage to face one of its ultimate and, as of now, foreseeable consequences: the placing of a group of elite troops without father or mother, without personal mooring, without any frame of reference with which to buttress a free and responsible personality, at the disposition of the Hitlers of tomorrow.

A series of questions ensues. Who will be served by this project? Who are the heirs of the Führer today? To what political uses will they put science and the most sophisticated biomedical techniques? What resources are today's scientists making available to the lords of the world? How will the priorities of research be determined? What programs will be paid for with particularly bountiful subsidies? Where will these subsidies come from? [24]

Whatever the replies to these questions, two things are certain. First, the lords of the world are prepared to practice indoctrination and ideological colonization on a planetary scale. This explains how, surrendering to what Toynbee called "Herodianism," today some people are able to sanction the practices for which, fifty years ago, Hitler was censured. . . Today's lords have available means in the biomedical field that Hitler could scarcely even envision, but whose first rumors he was aware of and able to exploit. Segregation and discrimination, artificial selection, positive and negative eugenics, sterilization, euthanasia: nothing has changed in the program except that the methods available are totally effective and pitiless in determination. And we won't even speak of the aftermath promised us in relatively short order.[25]

With the other choice, on the other hand, there is no reason for the change to be fatal, and this second alternative requires less development. Beyond being the embodiment of their history, common reference to the fundamental values of democracy is the strength of European peoples and the source of their unity. Certainly Europeans don't have a monopoly on democracy, but these values were affirmed among them first, at the cost of much blood and tears, and they will be loyal to it only to the degree that they continue to promote it on a universal scale.

In order to do this, they need not submit in any way to the edicts of any elite whatever. They are not committed to conceive of liberty according to the American model, nor of equality according to the Soviet model. Other avenues are open to them. Still, in any case, they simply must refuse all forms of heteronomy and alienation. To be clearer, they must refuse to collaborate in schemes of domination where they would also be the primary target.[26]

This is the price of their credibility for new generations and for the Third World.

11. TO BE CREDIBLE BEFORE THE THIRD WORLD

Here again European politicians are faced with a choice.

In one scenario, they may allow for a certain growth among developing nations, but one under strict control. They will be forced, then, to apply universally the population control methods supereffective among peoples of the Third World, and to adopt, on an intercontinental scale, the segregation, containment and selection policies extoled by Galton and others since the nineteenth century.[27] Today's facts confirm almost daily, as it were, that this tendency is being exploited by some, to be met only by a complacent murmur from many of our contemporaries.

Europeans may yet play this role of oppressors for the benefit of a center of power which will manipulate them, use them as a sort of relay, and over which they will have no influence or control.

In another scenario, if politicians admit that life, liberty and justice have merit and are desirable for them and their fellow citizens, then they must also admit that these have merit and are desirable for others. If these values are good for them, then they are good for every other human being as well. They will be obliged to share life, liberty and justice with all humanity. If, as F. Heer said, "Europe is the mother of revolutions," it is because she is aware that no individual, race, or nation can appropriate these values for its exclusive use. Europe has gradually discovered that what constitutes dignity is not the privilege of kings, nor that of nobility, nor that of the bourgeoisie. Europe is confronted once again by her destiny as the "mother of revolutions": to promote always unconditional respect for every human being within her boundaries and everywhere else in the world. Only thus will Europe be able again to define her worldwide, universal vocation.

It is also clear that there is an essential and , so to speak, necessary link between the attitude Europe adopts toward itself and the one it adopts toward the Third World.

12. CONCLUSION

In summary, we cannot build the future of democracy by endorsing a reversion to a morality of the species. Nor can we conceive of a such a policy as management of human cattle. We cannot found a happy society if happiness is the privilege of the strongest. We cannot build justice on a lie. Nor can we build peace on violence, whether structural, surgical or genetic.

It would be disastrous for Europe to venture onto the paths of a pan-Naziism, of which she would be both agent and victim.

In the face of all these dangers, it is high time to put up some resistance.[28]

Endnotes for Chapter IV

[1] Cf. Plato, *Gorgias* 482c - 486d.

[2] Cf. Aristotle, *Metaphysics* K6 1062b 12-15.

[3] Regarding the historical aspects of the problems to be met, we limit ourselves to cite: George H. Sabine, *A History of Political Theory*, 3rd ed. (London: Harrap, 1971); T. A. Sinclair, *Histoire de la pensée politique grecque* (Paris: Payot, 1953). On the Sophists the best reference is that of W. K. C. Guthrie (Paris: Payot, 1973).

[4] Cf. Plato, Meno 81e -82d.

[5] See Sophocles, *Antigone* v. 446 ff; *Oedipus Rex* v. 863 ff; Plato, *Apology; Crito* 44b-49e.

[6] Cf. Xenophon, *Memorabilia* 1, 2, 43; cited by Sinclair, op.cit 37.

[7] For all this see especially the Preamble of the Declaration.

[8] Tocqueville, *Democracy in America* I, II, 7.

[9] The specific character of totalitarianism has been the object of many recent studies. We mention only: Stanley Milgram, *Soumission à l'autorité* (Paris: Calmann-Levy, 1984); Christian Delacampagne, *Figures de l'oppression*, (Paris: Presses Universitaires de France, 1977); Jean-Jacques Walter, *Les machines totalitaires* (Paris: Presses Universitaires de France, 1977). We should not forget Etienne de La Boetie, *Le Discours de la servitude volontaire* (Paris: Payot, 1976).

[10] Sic! Simone Veil, *Exposé* published in Mexico 1977. *Intercontinental Population Conference*, 678 published by IUSSP in Liège. The quotation is found on page 598. On the place of the family in utopias see Igor Chafarevitch, *Le phénomène socialiste* (Paris: Seuil, 1977), passim, esp. 278-283/

[11] Cf. the *Republic* V, 460n-462a.

[12] We have analyzed the "doctrine of national security" in *Destin du Brésil. La technocratie militaire et son idéologie* (Gembloux: Duculot, 1973).

[13] Cf. Sun Tzu, *L'Art de la Guerre* (Paris: Flammarion, 1972).

[14] Cf. Plato's *Republic* 414b-415d.

[15] On the relationships between the lie and violence, see Hannah Arendt, *Du mensonge à la violence. Essai de politique contemporaine* (Paris: Calmann-Levy, 1972); Alexander Solzhenitsyn, *Lettre aux dirigeants de l'Union Soviétique* (Paris: Seuil, 1974), especially 127-133. See also Plato, *Phaedrus* 267d-268.

[16] The conclusions reached by Dr. Patricia Soutoul in her thesis merits being closely examined by the medical corps: see *L'information médicale continue du grand public en matière de reproduction humaine.*

[17] Democracy's precarious condition is well elucidated in Michel Crozier, Samuel P Huntington and Joji Watanuki's report, *The Crisis of Democracy* (New York: University Press, 1975), see esp. 115.

[18] See Pascal Diener, "Idée nominaliste et déconstruction du droit," in *Archives de philosophie du Droit* t. 28, *Philosophie pénale* (Paris: Sirey, 1983) 229-255.

[19] We take up this question in *Destin du Brésil* (Gembloux: Duculot, 1973) 50.

[20] See Ph. Caspar, *L'individuation des êtres* (Paris-Namur: Lethielleux, 1985).

[21] On this theme see a text especially thought provoking: Martin Heidegger in *Sein und Zeit*, 8th edition (Tübingen: Niemeyer, 1957) 26, esp. p. 122.

[22] For the special case of the medical corps, see Yves Ternon and Socrate Helman, *Les médecins allemands et le national-socialisme* (Tournai: Casterman, 1973). Regarding the intellectuals about the USSR, see David Caute, *Les compagnons de route* (Paris: Laffont, 1979). There is an important bibliography in both books. Plato himself had a strange conception of the relationships between medicine and politics; see *Republic* 405a - 410a.

[23] See Zbigniew Brzezinski, *Between Two Ages. America's Role in the Technetronic Era* (New York: Harmondsworth, 1978; 1st ed.: 1970).

[24] Some aspects of these problems are taken up in *Biology as a Social Weapon* issued by the Ann Arbor Science for the People Editorial Collective (Minneapolis, MN: Burgess, 1977). The complexity of the problem can be seen also in *Onzième rapport annuel de l'Organisation mondiale de la Santé* which presents the *Programme Spécial de recherche, de developpement et de formation à la recherche en reproduction humaine,* (Geneva, November 1982).

[25] See, for example, the interviews collected by Michel Salomon in *L'avenir de la vie* (Paris: Seghers, 1981).

[26] From among the abundant literature on the two models, we point out Yves Eudes, *La Conquête des esprits. L'appareil d'esportation culturelle americaine* (Maspero, 2983); Igor Chafarevitch, *Le phénomène socialiste*, op.cit. in note 10.

[27] Cf. among others Yvette Conry (ed.) *De Darwin au Darwinisme: science et idéologie. Congrès international pour le centenaire de la mort de Darwin*, Paris-Chantilly, Sept. 13-16, 1982 (Paris: Vrin, 1983).

[28] This is one of the central themes of Bernard-Henry Levy in *Le testament de Dieu* (Paris: Grasset, 1979).

chapter V

THE CHRISTIAN PRACTICE
OF ATHEISM

In another time, when a Christian climate still suffused society, if ever anyone began to neglect systemically his religious duties, to desert the churches, to fail to take off his hat as processions passed by, his acquaintances spontaneously traced the explanation for his behavior to an intellectual evolution. To act as though God did not exist meant that one had chosen a negative response to the *theoretical* question of God's existence.

The situation today is very different. Yes, man begins more often than not to act as though God did not exist, going along with the atmosphere of general permissiveness, with the surrounding mentality or the ideologies in the air. Then, one fine day, he draws theoretical conclusions.

This is precisely the dynamic affecting certain Christians who subscribe to the so-called "progressive" alternatives regarding bioethics and respect for life. This behavior is analogous to that of other Christians who, in fighting on a "common front," are exposed to becoming communists. This second attitude's effects will help us better to perceive the consequences of the first.

1. TO DENY GOD IN THOUGHT

Theoretical atheism, which consists of an intellectual choice that conditions behavior, goes back to antiquity. It went underground during the Middle Ages, only to surface again during the Renaissance, becoming bold and soon asserting itself in broad daylight.[1] We find materialist expressions of atheism that follow a tradition ranging from Lucretius to many "philosophers" of the eighteenth century, including, for example, Helvetius and Holbach. Atheism can equally be seen in the idealist tradition, and here call to mind the atheistic currents deriving from the thought of Spinoza and even Hegel.

In our era there flourish, above all, forms of atheism centered on man. These are strongly inspired by Feuerbach's thought, whose influence on the formation of Marx's thought was great. According to this philosopher, man must reclaim the essence that he was deprived of when he projected it onto a mythical being called God. Everything that man attributes to God, including existence, he does at the cost of mutilating himself. I deprive myself, dispossess myself, separate and alienate myself to whatever degree I affirm God, His existence and His nature. Man can extricate himself from this alienation only by taking back his destiny into his own hands. For man, reconciliation is to reappropriate the attributes he once ascribed to God.[2]

If it is indebted to the Hegelian tradition, Feuerbach's thought is just as indebted to the naturalist tradition with a strong pantheistic connotation, represented by Giordano Bruno then by Tommaso Campanella toward the end of the sixteenth century. Born in the climate of the Renaissance's humanism, this kind of atheism frequently ran with other forms of theoretical atheism, for example, in the corrosive thought of Bayle. Atheism is thus expressed in a wide array of manifestations: metaphysical, critical, humanist.

Apart from these different manifestations, theoretical atheism tends to make man the measure of all things. Man is cut off from his existential dependence on God the provident creator — even if reference to the Great Architect, conceived in a vague and imprecise manner, is maintained. In short, if man is the measure of all things, he will also be the measure of God and, if possible, the measure of other men.

Some present-day problems echo the secular discussions that Renan, Le Dantec, Berthelot and others tried to revive.[3] It is in this complex ground that the different forms of contemporary atheism take root, whether it be Camus' humanist variety or Pierre Simon's scientist one. We have spoken of the latter in the preceding chapters. Furthermore, in the unstable currents of very diverse kinds of atheism, we see pseudo-religions flourish: the "religion" of man, the "religion" of science, etc.

Nonetheless, these different varieties of atheism have enjoyed but a handful of initiates in attendance. In fact, discussions about the logical foundation of atheism are hardly of interest to the public at large. They are regarded as too heady; so even the most militant atheists avoid promoting their cause through a negative catechesis about God, a sort of "atheology."

2. TO DENY GOD THROUGH ACTION

In fact, atheistic proselytism has found in our day a much more effective mode for expansion. Disguised as pluralism, as the free disposition of one's body, as the right to experiment, as "sincerity," etc., everywhere it endeavors to impose its life-style, its sentiments, its way of being, acting and reacting. It is in practice that it tries to persuade man to take complete control of himself and his life. Sartre, in particular, familiarized us with the foolish concept of individual liberty as having no limits, no responsibility, and no end. As our analysis reveals, this concept of liberty only strengthened the influence of the materialist tradition.

From that point forward they no longer argue from positions tending to show that God does not exist, that he is "inconceivable," et cetera. Instead, they exploit themes such as the "autonomy" of man, among others, and replace rational arguments with affective and sentimental arguments. It matters little if there is a God, they suggest; the question is of no interest. What matters is to live today. Men thus are urged to act, then to think, without any other point of reference than themselves, without any other concern than what is useful to them. This has been the source, especially for certain Christians, of a total indifference to any teaching of the Church's Magisterium. To be more specific, an ethic of trespass emerges: since neither fault nor sin exist, there is no longer place for salvation.

Profound problems are systematically pushed into the shadows, while immediate efficacy and short-term benefits bathe in the limelight. In these circumstances, man finds it easy to auto-justify and auto- confirm the opinions that he himself validates by his conduct before others.

3. REPROCESSED CHRISTIANS

A typical example of this occurs in the political arena. Political alliances typically induce Christians to adopt Marxist behavior that ends by emptying their faith of any concrete impact, and even, at the end of the process, by rendering this faith vain, useless. Dogmatic questions are but parenthetical and declared uninteresting in the face of the great revolutionary project, which calls for all to join forces in a common front. A generous soul, seduced by the project, does not always perceive that the most beautiful words can lead to very different realities, and that in the mouth of a communist, everything is good, proper, and fraternal if the Cause wins.

The Christian then begins to fight for an ideal that is not his own except in appearance; his actions are void of any specific content; his vocabulary, now equivocal, is occupied little by little by his partners' meanings. The very terms of theological language are reprocessed and then serve as a cutting blade in ideological subjugation. The words now function according to a strange, alienating logic. The coming of the Kingdom of God, for example, is defined within a purely worldly, materialist framework.

The next step is to confine religion and its supernatural and cultural aspects to a strictly private sphere, and to deem it a disincarnate, purely contemplative affair, without any influence in life, without any effect on real situations. In short, it is the dead faith referred to by St. James.

From then on, there is no longer place for a Christian sense of action, or for specifically Christian action. An authoritative word from the Church is no longer sought. The message of the Magisterium becomes insignificant and Christian witness superfluous. Why should this witness be expressed only in specifically Christian institutions? The idea of pluralism, which is full of traps, justifies the dissolution of all Christian points of reference. At this stage, Christians find themselves to be objectively communists and atheists, even if subjectively they feel that they are still Christian.[4]

4. MASTERS WITHOUT GOD

It is the same regarding life. Some of the conduct in the matter of abortion, euthanasia, genetic manipulation, etc., leads slowly but surely to atheism by the very fact that Christians adopt it. Whoever acts as though he does not have to welcome every man simply because he *is*, as though he does not have to respect him or seek his welfare, as though he were not absolutely responsible for him; whoever acts as though he can decide on life or death for his neighbor and even use him for expedient and selfish interests; whoever acts as though, according to his means, he is radically the master of the other's destiny as well as of his own, free to call to life or to kill, without a norm to follow or an account to render, with no other point of reference but himself — how can such a person still look upon himself and all his brothers as being sons of the Father who loves them, shows them what is good, and how to attain it?

A man cannot reasonably maintain that his destiny lies outside himself, in the eternal dialogue with God, who is introduced to man through his dialogue with his brothers, and at the same time refuse to acknowledge the other in his actions, or does so only when considered to his advantage. In summoning every sort of doubt, then even making decisions over his own death, a man cannot still accept the slightest dominion over his life from a loving Providence.

It is very difficult to deny that our society's choices concerning fertility and population control by any means — abortion, euthanasia, genetic manipulation — reflect and propagate a mindset that is incompatible with Christ's message.[5] Even when well intentioned, the Christian who adopts these ways of acting will necessarily end in sanctioning the ideology behind them.

5. THE NEW BETRAYAL BY INTELLECTUALS

Respect for all human life from the moment of its origin is at the heart of the Gospel message, just as it is true that every human being's primordial act of recognition comes from God and not from man, and that all humans are the object of their Creator and Savior's desire, One who wishes to offer us the free choice to enter into a relationship of love with Him. By denying this through their actions, some Christians reject an essential point of their doctrine. But a more grave step is taken when theorists attempt to conceal the contradiction by means of a biased presentation of the practice and by an interpretation of the Gospel message that is a betrayal of its meaning and spirit (2 Cor 4:2). For that, it suffices to relativize the content of the words. . .

While some Christian intellectuals in Latin America, South Africa and elsewhere make it a point of honor to denounce prophetically whatever oppresses or destroys man, especially "the smallest," in the West we see others who get involved in endorsing techniques that call for the radical oppression of a whole category of human beings.

They have taken on an extremely serious responsibility. Not only do they strive to empty the life-giving word of Scripture and Tradition of its substance, but also to transform dogma and morality into accomplices of domination by the powerful. In this way they participate in generating some of the most sophisticated forms of totalitarianism that threaten future generations.

These intellectuals, doubtlessly unaware, set a process of undermining of the ecclesial community into motion. They teach skepticism instead of the Magisterium in Christian circles. They undermine the *consensus fidelium* in one capital point of the Gospel — the absolute respect for every human being. They make the most "progressive" biotechnological practices acceptable in Christian clinics, social service agencies, schools, universities, parties and unions.

When these theorists defend and permit practices in Christian institutions that derive objectively from practical atheism, plainly it is the Church they are assailing.

When they virtually empty these institutions of their specifically Christian character, they attack the sole means available to the community of faithful through which their actions are endowed with historical effectiveness. They impugn the very possibility of witness from the Christian community as such, thereby accustoming people to the mentality that religion is a matter of personal devotion that has no impact on concrete sociohistorical reality, and is quite capable of doing without institutional support.

And thus it is all sewn up. Those who contribute to the self-destruction of the Church will also dig the grave of the faith, since Christians necessarily receive this faith *from* and *in* the Church, whose whole *raison d'être* is to assemble the community and offer the divine gifts of the Word and the Bread to her members.

If these theories end in producing such a deleterious result for the faith, it is because from their very point of departure they were contrary to it. Who cannot recognize that their premise is that man wants to receive his sense of self exclusively from himself, or rather from those "enlightened" ones, without any reference to a law from his Creator?

6. LEVIATHAN AND PROMETHEUS

It is clear that this deviation from Christianity that endorses objectively atheistic practices, has the same source as the most virulent forms of contemporary atheism. This latter tends less to draw out the consequences of God's absence than to seek to control of the idol that obsesses it: the blasphemous image of a God jealous of His creature. Twentieth century atheism considers itself to be in chains, the toy of a capricious divinity; it seems to want to free itself by "taking the fire away from Zeus." In order to affirm itself, this school of thought tries to mimic God, to steal what is proper to Him, to appropriate His essence.

It cannot be denied that some of our biotechnicians' tinkerings, full of both ingenuity and contempt, proceed from this implacable will to conquer heaven, to succeed where Icarus failed so lamentably.

This god that man wants to be for himself is but a mortal god. Like Leviathan, the biblical monster that is master over the seas and all its creatures, he wants to be all-powerful and yet must die. Although he is having a good time amusing himself; although like a new Narcissus he is bewitched by his own prowess, he can see on the horizon of his existence the inescapable specter of death. And so, resenting his failure at mastering life, his own life, he gives in to one last blaze of pride by wanting to master death. At the end of a diabolical alchemy, man, once cooperator with God in the enterprise of life, is transformed into a collaborator with Satan as an agent of death.

The psalms proclaim that all nature manifests the Creator. But in all of nature, from among all other creatures, man is the closest to God. Of all creation, man is, from his most hidden origins, the resplendent image of God par excellence. This is why, as Scripture tells us, Satan is a liar and a murderer, after the fashion of Prometheus and Leviathan.[6] He is the enemy of life, the enemy of human life, because of all of the created world, man is the endlessly refracted image of God's generosity.

Hence, if human life no longer speaks of the Creator, how can man's death be a passage to God, following Him whom the Father made the firstborn from the dead?

Prometheus and Leviathan thus wind up lost in the same nonsense, shattered by the same pride, foundering in the same despair. After attempting to take away our life, witness how they now join in stealing our death. The death they offer us is no longer a death of passage, no longer the Paschal death, but death as a dead-end that is, a priori, closed to even the idea of resurrection.

There is no truce possible between these two monsters, Prometheus and Leviathan, and God the Father, the God of life and friend of man, revealed by Jesus Christ. No one can serve two masters. . .

Endnotes for Chapter V

[1] Cf. Jean Lacroix, *Le sens de l'athéisme moderne*, 3rd ed. (Tournai: Casterman, 1961).

[2.] We studied this problem in *Démocratie et libération chrétienne*, 109-125 and passim.

[3] On this point it is always useful to consult Ph. Cremer, "Savant et croyant," *L'Humanisme scientifique devant la foi*, No. 707, March 1975 (Brussels: Ed. La Pensée catholique).

[4] The process spoken of here is analyzed more closely in *Démocratie et libération chrétienne*, 100-108.

[5] Cf. *ibid*. 125-133.

[6] See Jn 6:44.

chapter VI

TWENTY THESES
BY WAY OF CONCLUSION

To close our study, certain crucial conclusions stand out. They allow us to see what we are rushing toward. Suffice to mention these conclusions briefly in the form of theses:

1) Extremely grave *political problems* hide behind the problems presented by doctors as arising from individual treatment.

2) Due to lack of attention to this political dimension, biomedical problems are generally presented in the reverse. The masses are kept busy with a casuistry that is constantly recycled with every new exploit. Thus the essential question remains eclipsed: *what kind of society do we want to build?*

3) The legislation liberalizing abortion seems to be limited to a specific area. In reality, however, it brings about a change in the *nature* of democratic society, a mutation that causes democracy to tend toward totalitarianism.

4) The first *victims* of this shift are the frailest of human beings: those just conceived and those not yet born. Then there are the women, wounded in body and heart, to whom oppression is presented as emancipation. As for the men — often the agents of this change, always the beneficiaries — they are also mentally subjugated.

5) In the end, the threat hanging over the most frail will hang over all men. Active *euthanasia*, practiced at the prenatal stage out of utility, will be extended to other categories of human beings for analogous reasons.

6) In vitro fertilization also obviously poses the question of respect for the human individual. It raises problems that bear many different consequences. I.V.F. opens wide the way for the breakup of the *family*; it destroys natural bonds before they can even develop. It sends man back to his aloneness, thereby making him an especially vulnerable being.

7) Up to now, even the fiercest forms of totalitarianism have never succeeded in destroying the family, and the family has always been a *bastion* of resistance against totalitarianism. The twenty-first century's forms of totalitarianism need not even be concerned about the family anymore, since biocrats will already have taken care of that.

8) *Information* on these questions, from the properly biomedical point of view as well as that of politics, is censored or distorted as necessary. The complexity of the problems allows for the abuse of the public and the concealment of highest truths.

9) An entire *ideological apparatus* that exploits the human rights issue as well as the development issue, aims at deluding people about the true ethical and political perils of the practices to which they want to accustom people.

10) Thus, over and above surgical and genetic violence, there is *ideological violence* done to man's intelligence and will. Through the perversion of intelligence and redirection of the will, this most basic violence is done to the personality. It is simply a matter of convincing men to agree to their own enslavement.

11) Toward this end, they spread the *fear* of overpopulation — with its corollary, the obsession with *defense*. This element is parallel to the one invoked to justify the recourse to nuclear weapons, but now "nuclear defense" is substituted by "demographic defense" and "biological defense," with the implacable efficiency these call for.

12) Thus we witness a *new alliance* between violence and the lie. The target is the "I," in body and mind. This monstrous alliance signals the emergence of the most sophisticated totalitarianism ever imagined.

13) *Biologists* and *doctors*, as exposed as all men to ideological colonization, are directly threatened with becoming accomplices of this terrible alliance — as agents and/or beneficiaries.

14) To the extent that they give in to this complicity, specialists in medical sciences *alter* medicine's very nature. Hippocrates estab-

lished the interpersonal relationship between physician and patient; but henceforth, medicine will become an instrument of power at the service of totalitarianism.

15) A similar situation threatens *other intellectuals* as well: demographers, agronomists, publicists, politicians, etc.

16) Because of their effectiveness, current biomedical resources allow for the *quantitative and qualitative control* of world population, and generalized *eugenics* looms on the horizon. Due their numbers and races, Third World countries should be the first ones to be concerned about these prospects of control.

17) Through faulty judgment, some ideologically colonized Christians naively embark on the disastrous paths of *practical atheism*. God, dethroned by Prometheus, is chased away from Christian action. Man wants to be himself with total autonomy, radically alienating him from his Creator.

18) Some Christian theorists, seeking to justify atheistic practices objectively, in fact *lend power to this alienation*. They drain the Bible and Tradition of an essential part of their meaning. They remove from Christian institutions everything specifically Christian, thus putting dogma and morality at the service of the powerful.

19) By the same token, they deny the truth of the twofold prophetic endeavor of the Church: the promotion of human rights on a universal scale and the preferential but not exclusive option for the poorest. They render the Church *ineffective*, as well as the Word of Life she announces.

20) In sum, biocratic power over life entails the subjugation of man's intelligence and will. *Total control* over humankind is its final consequence.